To Aunt Pat,   June, 2019

Thank you for your

beautiful **Loss** heart---

for all the "butterfly

love," the *Light* support and

encouragement you've shown

Illuminating the Path Through Grief

me, especially in these

last four years!" I love

you and am so grateful

that you're in my (and mom's)

Karen Trench

life! Blessings Always,

Karen

The Song of the Phoenix

What can be said about you in truth is unknown,
but still you hearten long-wearied worlds with
the idea that we can rise again from dear things destroyed.
What form are you?
What color?
I think the story tellers have taken their
liberties with what is visible, while leaving the great
sages to contemplate despair, wonderment, joy
and other unsleepable things that cannot be seen.
What calls out to you to do as you do for
five hundred years at a turn without reward
or even the acrid scent of mercy?
Ashes to ashes, note the most trusted scribes,
Till thou return unto the ground;
For out of it wast thou taken:
for dust thou are, and unto dust
shalt thou return,
though they didn't realize that it was you
at the time of scripture.
your entombment and decay,
teachings, warnings, reckonings:
we must not diminish the ancestor's

departing blessedness for the ancestor is the
vessel from which new life emerges.
So must say the toad of the tadpole,
the tree of the seed,
the man of his mother,
the woman of this earth, and
the earth of something wordless.
I've never heard spoken of your song,
but recently I learned it
as it glided, breathlessly,
across my own vocal chords
in response to some beckoning
from above.
It seems that I am the Life that
has been left behind.

Jamie K. Reaser, 2019

First edition: April 2019

Editing by Laurie Viera Rigler
Cover design by Michael Molinet
Interior Design by Raven Dodd
Author Photograph by Julie Sylvester, 29:11 Photography

Additional information and resources may be found at:
www.karentrench.com

ISBN: 9780578477763
Library of Congress Control Number: 2019904248

Imprint: Independently published by: KT Publishing, LLC

Contents

Foreword

Grief never comes invited. It takes no effort on our part. We who bear grief didn't stay up at night wishing it on ourselves, or wishing our dear ones to be so far away for so long. Grief finds us, along with the entourage of emotional, physical and spiritual changes that ensue. Yet despite the ubiquity of loss, it never seems to show up in predictable ways.

Grief arrives in our lives on its own terms.

Healing on the other hand, must be invited. Unlike grief, healing requires effort and a deliberate strategy. And unlike grief, healing is not universal. The pain of loss can change us.

One of the hard truths for many people who suffer grief is that it simply doesn't go away. It can change, alternating from subtle to more acute grief depending on the time of year, the people we are with, or not with, or the music we listen to. Grief doesn't usually have an on-off switch like we wish it could, even though many of us become skilled at hiding our pain.

So many of us carry on in our human existence with unhealed pain that comes to define who we are, who we think ourselves to be. Healing demands from each of us that we do things differently once we experience the pain of loss. We often have to step outside of our comfort zones that grief has already shaken. And often, we have to change our ideas of what healing is in order to be able to hold our pain.

Each of us has our own unique experience with grief and healing. None of us do either quite the same. However, Karen Trench has constructed a manual from her own experience of pain. Part of what makes this book you are reading so helpful is that it allows you to contemplate from the starting point of loss many different way to facilitate healing. This is no simplistic feel-good book. There is anguish on each page, that same bottomless immensity that I am sure you have felt. My feeling is that you will resonate with the emotions she is sharing—the feeling of loss, of missing something, of a sense of always being out of step. But my hope is that you will also resonate with the recommendations that come in the form of what she calls "blessings."

Why blessings? Is there such a thing as a blessing in the magnitude of grief?

I believe so, because it's often in places of great pain that we find the value of our precious human lives. Our capacity to love, share and feel together—all of them are done almost automatically until our lives are shaken by unthinkable losses. Karen has brought her experience into light to share with you the possibility of healing, even if it's just a little bit. And as many of you have experienced, when people go out of their way to use their human capacity to care to address the bottomless suffering of grief, it is indeed a blessing.

This book will not make grief go away. This book can show you how to hold the grief in your life from a loving place. Loss feels so punishing and so alone. Holding yourself gently, lovingly, when you are suffering—perhaps that's what your loved one would do? Allow this book to do the same.

Sameet Kumar, Ph.D.
Coral Gables, FL

Author, Grieving Mindfully, The Mindful Path Through Worry and Rumination, and Mindfulness for Prolonged Grief.

xii

The Sweet Taste of Grief

I saw grief drinking from a cup of sorrow
and called out,
"It tastes sweet, does it not?"
"You've caught me," grief answered,
"And you have ruined my business.
How can I sell sorrow
when you know it's a blessing?"

Rumi

I

Lessons Learned

"Pay attention, the Beloved is whispering, 'Loss teaches you everything.' " Alfred K. LaMotte

WHEN I WAS A TEENAGER, I dreamed of one day penning the Great American Novel. What I never dreamed is that I would one day write the book you are now holding. Maybe it's human to go through life thinking that bad things happen only to other people. Such magical thinking worked for me until the day fate came knocking at my door.

One fine spring day in 2015, my beloved husband of twenty-three years took his own life. I'd had no warning. I was completely clueless. His sudden departure was utterly shocking and devastating. In truth, it almost destroyed me. In an effort to acknowledge and release my emotions, I began writing a grief journal to help me heal. My journal became the cornerstone of this book.

Author Isak Dinesen, who bore a great deal of sorrow in her own life, wrote in her book Out of Africa, "All sorrows can be borne if you put them into or tell a story about them." Writing my story about the tragic loss of my husband is a way to further lighten the load of sorrow that, after nearly four years, presses against my still healing heart. My fervent wish is that it helps to lighten yours too.

You will notice that I often quote from the many books about grief and loss I read during my darkest times. These books were my salvation and helped to keep me sane. They were something for me to hold on to when I felt most alone.

When my journey through grief began, I looked upon my sudden loss as a curse. My heart had been broken open, laid bare, exposed, and vulnerable. I was literally prostrate with grief. I thought it inconceivable that it could bestow upon me even one blessing, let alone multiple ones. But as I read and wrote and healed, I came to realize that I was much stronger than I ever imagined. And as time unfolded and I recovered, the grieving process gave me many valuable insights and lessons. I began to uncover golden nuggets of truth about myself and about life that had been buried before my loss. I came to see these as blessings and treasured them because each served to transform me in positive ways. I also came to understand that this experience was not sanctioning my loss but rather was a way of honoring both my husband and myself.

As Kathryn Walker says in her book *A Stopover in Venice*, "Rich and mysterious gifts are concealed in the dark folds of pain." For me, this knowing came only with time. When it comes to grieving, some things must wait until our hearts can bear it.

I determined early on that as insurmountable as it felt, I was going to walk headlong into my towering wall of grief. Although walking around that wall would have been far easier, I was possessed with a deeper knowing—far beyond intuition—that told me if I took the shortcut, I was never going to heal and that sooner or later, my grief would most surely manifest in an unhealthy manner. And as the great Winston Churchill once said, "If you're going through hell, keep going."

And so, I kept going.

Although my husband took his own life, this book is not about suicide or being a suicide survivor per se. *Love Loss Light* depicts my step-by-step journey through grief and is my way of sharing with you the many blessings that were bestowed upon me while on my quest to heal my heart. Little by little, these blessings began to fill up and illuminate all of those dark, empty places in my heart and soul and ultimately led me back to living and loving life again. If but one of them can give you even one measure of comfort as you walk your own path, then I have learned my lessons well.

No journey through loss and grief is the same, but each journey can inform another's. No one gets out of this life— this gift of having a human experience—unscathed. Pain, loss, and suffering are part of the gift of being human. There is no way to avoid it. Having walked my path for close to four years now, I have learned well that it is the brought-to-your-knees experiences that teach us the most valuable lessons. That everything in life is transient. That our good and bad experiences are all fleeting. That this too shall pass. And, finally, that our lives are so precious—each and every moment is a gift to be cherished and embraced because nothing lasts forever except one thing—and that is love. Love is the heartbeat of all of creation. Love is eternal and everlasting. Love never dies, ever! Love is the greatest blessing of all.

So lean into the wind and just keep going, knowing this: It is our love that leads us to grief, but it is our grief that leads us back to love.

I dedicate this book to you.

"There is no end. For the soul there is never birth nor death, nor, having once been, does it ever cease to be. It is unborn, eternal, ever-existing, undying and primeval. It is not slain when the body is slain."
Bhagavad-Gita

Karen Trench

Bitter Sweet Resonance

I have been honed by pain
as the fine resonate cello
is honed by time—
and grief has kissed my face
leaving its mark upon my brow
changing forever my vision
sweetly, ever so sweetly opening
my heart.

Catherine Firpo, 1989

Karen Trench

2

The Journey Begins

Karen Trench

"How shall my heart be unsealed, unless it be broken?" Kahlil Gibran

MY JOURNEY THROUGH GRIEF began the day after Easter at approximately 6:30 p.m., Monday, April 6, 2015. I suspected something had happened to my husband, Charlie, when he didn't arrive home that afternoon for an important telephone conference with his business associates. We were to eat dinner very early that day, at 3:00 p.m., and then he'd get on his scheduled call at 4 p.m. Charlie and I were one of those glued-at-the-hip couples and had been since we'd first met almost twenty-three years earlier. We lived, loved, and worked together. We were best friends. If either of us was going to be late arriving home for any reason, we would always call to let each other know. I couldn't recall one time in all our years together when this wasn't the case ... except for this day. When 3 p.m. turned into 3:30 p.m., I knew instinctively something was wrong.

By 4 p.m., and after about a dozen failed attempts to reach him on his mobile, all the alarms were going off in my head. Charlie was punctual. In all the years I'd known him, he had never, in my recollection, missed either an in-person meeting or a scheduled conference call, especially an important one. I knew this about Charlie, and so did his longtime business associate, Vic. When Vic couldn't raise Charlie on his phone after repeated attempts, he called me and expressed deep concern that something had to have happened to him. He offered to call all the area hospitals to see if someone fitting Charlie's description had been admitted.

By now, I was frantic and called my younger sister, Kathy, to tell her what was going on. Without hesitation, she jumped into her car and headed to my house, about a thirty-minute drive away. Before hanging up with me, Kathy's wife, Sharon, grabbed the phone and gave me the number of my county's non-emergency police line and told me to start there. I made the call immediately upon hanging up with her.

I wasn't feeling hopeful that I'd glean any information, but I was wrong—and what I heard nearly paralyzed me with fear. The dispatcher told me that yes, there had been an "incident" involving my husband but that she couldn't give me too many details, except to ask if he'd had an appointment that day with the VA hospital in Denver. I was taken aback. Charlie was a Vietnam veteran and did receive medical care through the VA hospital, but I knew that he did not have a scheduled doctor's appointment that day so I told her no. However, he had told me that he had scheduled a last-minute appointment with an individual who was involved with him in a secondary business venture, and the location of that meeting wasn't more than twenty minutes down the road. That's where I believed he had been. She took my number and said that she'd have someone who was more familiar with "the case" get back to me as soon as possible.

I was completely mystified. Why would she ask about the VA? How would she have known anything about Charlie's association with the VA hospital? After I hung up, I ran upstairs to our office and sat at Charlie's desk. He'd left his Outlook calendar open on his monitor, and I saw the name of the person he was supposed to be meeting with. I frantically dialed the number on the screen, but the person who answered, the person who Charlie *said* he was meeting, told me that no such meeting had been scheduled. After hanging up with him, I called Vic back and gave him the bleak update and promised I'd call him as soon as I knew more.

By the time Kathy arrived, I was in panic mode, so she took charge. She immediately called the Denver VA hospital, but the person who answered told her that no one by his name had been admitted to that facility. Kathy called other area hospitals and even jails, but to no avail. She then decided that another call to the original dispatcher I'd spoken with was warranted. The dispatcher informed her that there was now a detective on the case. A detective? The first thought that came to me was inconceivable: Had Charlie been murdered? Kathy begged the dispatcher to have this detective call us immediately, telling her, "My sister is going crazy with not knowing! We need to know something NOW! It's been over two hours!" I could hardly contain myself, and Kathy could hardly contain me.

Before I met Charlie, he had bought a beautiful log cabin in a fairly remote area off the grid at 9,000 feet in the Colorado Rockies. For security and protection, he'd also bought firearms: a handgun, a shotgun, and a rifle. In all the years we were together, I never saw him take one of them out, either at the cabin—where I later lived with him for a number of years—or in the home we now shared in the suburbs—where the guns, along with his guitar and our fireproof safe deposit box, were stored under the bed in our guest room.

I have absolutely no recollection of saying this, but Kathy insists that I said, "We need to go upstairs and check to see if Charlie's handgun is there because I think he may have committed suicide." It was as though this "knowing" had come to me, not by my own volition but instead transmitted through the ethers of the Universe from someone or something on high. Steeling ourselves, we made our way upstairs and sat together on the bedroom floor. My entire body convulsed in pure terror and dread as I dragged the gun box from under the bed and opened it.

His gun was gone.

My heart froze. I think I knew in that instant, and I believe Kathy did as well, that Charlie was never coming home. But she did point out that the clip of bullets was still there and that maybe Charlie hid the gun somewhere else in the house separate from the bullets. It was a very thin thread of hope to cling to, but we did.

The thread snapped when a short time later, the telephone rang. Kathy held my hand as I picked up the receiver. I will never forget the love I felt flowing from her hand to mine. The moment I picked up the phone, the person I'd been and the life I'd lived for the last twenty-three years disappeared. A detective from the Denver Police Department was on the other end saying words I could barely comprehend. It was as if he were talking from inside a tunnel and all I could hear was an echo. My ears couldn't grasp his words; they sounded so far away. But I did hear these words very clearly: "I am so sorry to have to tell you this, but your husband, Charlie, took his own life this afternoon." He went on to say something about how sorry he was to have told me over the phone but he knew that I'd been anxious for some news and he hadn't wanted to keep me waiting a minute longer.

I had received the call that everyone dreads. The call that changes one's life forever. I collapsed in a heap on the floor and let out a scream that seemed to emanate from the very bowels of the earth, a primordial scream that, looking back, I couldn't imagine came from me. I writhed in agony, bellowing out the word "no" over and over and over again. Kathy grabbed the phone and continued talking with the detective. He said that Charlie had taken his own life outside the VA hospital in Denver and that the cause of death was a self-inflicted gunshot wound. His death certificate would list his time of death as 15:15:15 military time, or 3:15 p.m. MST. While I was watching some mindless program on TV, eating our pasta dinner alone, my husband was already dead. Vic would later tell me that one of the local television news programs had reported a suspected suicide at the Denver VA hospital that afternoon and that in his gut he knew the victim was Charlie. I'm grateful we were spared hearing the report while trying to learn his fate.

I felt outside of myself as I rolled around the floor in a pool of emotional pain so all-encompassing that I couldn't, and still can't, fathom its depth. I remember Kathy's distraught face as she leaned over me, pleading with me to breathe ... to just keep breathing ... and telling me that she didn't want to lose me too. She would later tell me that she was fearful I would simply fade away on her as she frantically dialed the phone, first to call our mom in Connecticut and then our older sister in New Mexico. My then 87-year-old mom later told me that she would never forget the sounds emanating in the background from her precious daughter, the screams of abject agony and disbelief, and how helpless she felt being so far away.

Miraculously, and so like her, Kathy tamped down her fear for me and her own shock and sadness over losing her beloved brother-in-law to make more calls—to Charlie's son, brother, and sister and many more later on—as calmly as she could in the midst of complete chaos. She is a remarkable woman, and I was and will forever be so thankful that she was there by my side when I got the call. I will also be forever grateful to her, God,[1] and Universe that I will never have to know what it would have been like for me had she not been there at that moment. She is my earth angel. In the ensuing weeks, she would share with me her belief that she witnessed the old me leaving my body. I don't know if that's what it was, but I do know that in that moment, the person I'd been vanished completely.

It was as if my whole body cracked wide open, and the very essence of the person I was stored within that vessel poured out into infinity. Every molecule that *was* me was completely rearranged. In an instant, I was completely empty, devoid of anything that had once defined me and my

---

[1] Throughout the book, whenever and wherever I use words to describe my understanding of "God"—i.e., Higher Power, Holy Spirit, Source, Universe, The Divine, The One—please feel free to substitute any word(s) you would prefer depending on your own religious and/or spiritual beliefs. It is my belief that no matter the label, there is only "The One."

life. And in that moment, I surrendered to the absolute knowing that my life had just been inexorably altered and that I was now a different person on an entirely different journey. What filled up my now empty vessel was grief; every pore, every molecule of my being—heart, mind, body, and soul—was invaded with overwhelming grief. The last thought I remember having before the shock set in was that I was now a blank slate and that it was going to be solely up to me to find a way to reimagine life beyond the unimaginable.

Finding Solace in Words

I was brought to my knees and I was desperate to find solace, to find some scrap of meaning in my loss and suffering. For me, as it no doubt is for you, it was a matter of survival. For widows and widowers in particular, it literally can be a matter of survival, as we are most susceptible to what is known as the "widowhood effect." Various studies have shown that there is a clear causal effect between the death of a spouse and the mortality rate of the surviving partner, especially within the first six months of loss: up to forty percent of the partners pass away. I didn't want to die. Knowing both of these things opened me up to explore any and all methods of self-care—any book, any healer, almost any healing modality that would ease my suffering even in the slightest way.

My quest for relief became a spiritual quest, and it began with reading over forty books (within the first five months) on grief and loss and on mindfulness practice. I spent countless time and a bit of money on Amazon searching out books that I felt would help me, and then I would devour them. Just about every one of them gave me solace and comfort, knowing that I was not alone and that most of us, sooner or later, will need to fill the void left behind when someone we love dies.

Also within the first few months, a flyer appeared in my mailbox from The Great Courses advertising a course on CD called The Science of Mindfulness: A Research-Based Path to Well-Being. One of the tutorials within the course caught my attention, as it dealt with "mindfulness grieving." Those lectures introduced me to a book that would become my bible and is one I have since given and recommended to both family and friends in their time of grief: *Grieving Mindfully* by Sameet M. Kumar, PhD, a psychotherapist and a Buddhist. In particular, I took great comfort in his discussion of the impermanence of all things, including grief. The most beneficial tool I came away with, though, was the practice of mindfulness. It was largely because of this book that I learned the wisdom of turning toward the pain of my own grief and honoring it with self-compassion, attention, and willingness. This allowed me to just let my feelings be and to connect with the experience of grieving as it unfolded ... to always allow what *is* to just *be*.

Grief turns us inward. It gives us an opportunity to go deep within ourselves, to question life and to find purpose and meaning after loss. Unless and until I was willing to dive deeply into my suffering and "sit" with it, I would find no pearls. Dr. Kumar's book and its gift of mindfulness were blessings.

"The packed blackness of our sorrow suddenly sprouts bejeweled graces."
Alfred K. LaMotte

Finding Solace in Touch and Tears

After reading *Grieving Mindfully*, I began exploring Eastern philosophies and holistic healing modalities. Frequently, I was guided in serendipitous ways to many different healers and a traditional and wonderful psychologist and life coach. Today, after almost four years, I still employ the benefits of many of these holistic remedies. One of the first healing modalities I was guided to was massage therapy. Charlie and I had always been very affectionate with each other. We kissed and hugged every day, and each morning, we'd spoon together in bed. I was still in shock and disbelief when it dawned on me that I'd never again be able to touch him or be touched by him. This horrifying realization pushed me further into a downward spiral of deep, deep pain and longing. In that first week, I actually asked my sister Priscilla and her daughter Meghan to spoon with me in bed as Charlie used to do. Knowing this was a short-term remedy, not to mention a bit awkward all around, Meghan suggested massage therapy and proceeded to research and find a grief masseuse, Edye, who would come to my home. Edye had lost her daughter from a drug overdose only a year prior and began offering her in-home service when she herself was in the throes of grief and couldn't find anyone to administer to her needs in the same way.

Love, empathy, and profound compassion emanated through Edye's gifted hands, and her touch instantly helped liberate a deep well of anguish. I cried my way through many massages in the early days of grieving, but the touch and the tears aided me tremendously in my healing.

To this day, I am a firm believer in massage, especially deep-tissue massage. It is an important component to maintaining one's overall emotional and physical well-being. It helps to purify and cleanse us by releasing toxins from the body and from the soul. And while I may not be crying as much or as deeply while on the table as I used to do, I am sometimes still moved to tears.

"To weep is to make less the depth of grief."
William Shakespeare from King Henry VI, Part 3

Researchers have found that our tears contain chemicals with natural pain-relieving substances and help to cleanse the body of substances that accumulate under stress. Grieving debilitates us both emotionally and physically; it is enormously exhausting and stressful. So, we must never, ever hold back our tears, for they are necessary and healing. And when we cry, we must give ourselves permission to cry with our whole, tender, broken, and beautiful heart. A good cry truly does cleanse our soul.

"There is a sacredness in tears. They are not the mark of weakness, but of power. They speak more eloquently than ten thousand tongues. They are the

messengers of overwhelming grief and unspeakable love."
Washington Irving

Finding Balance

In her book, *Death and the Family: The Importance of Mourning*, author Lily Pincus writes, "When I asked an orthopedic surgeon who treated me whether people often fracture bones after bereavement, he said, without even looking up from my injured foot, 'Naturally. People lose their sense of balance.'" After Charlie died, I lost my sense of balance entirely. Like someone aboard a ship who hasn't yet gotten their sea legs, my knees shook constantly. My legs felt unusually heavy and weak, and I couldn't walk in a straight line for months. My stairs presented a real challenge. I held the banister tightly going both up and down, and took the stairs one at a time.

When I shared this with Edye, she told me that the same thing had happened to her when her daughter passed and that she'd found an energy healer, Holly, who helped her tremendously with this symptom and who could also treat me at my home. Through the use of crystal healing and Reiki, Holly helped to open up my chakras, the seven energy centers in our body through which energy flows: the root, the sacral, the solar plexus, the heart, the throat, the third eye, and the crown of the head—all of which, according to her, had "been completely blown" by shock. Although it would take months, her healing modality went a long way to calm my chronically shaky legs and to restore my sense of balance and equilibrium. Edye and Holly were but two of the many gifted healers that I was blessed to have been guided to early on.

Even after my sense of balance had been restored, the aftereffects of shock lingered. The most difficult challenge I was plagued with right from the start was my inability to concentrate fully on anything substantive for any length of time. I couldn't stay focused on or follow the thread of conversations, making it almost impossible to remember what had been said to me—or worse, what I might have said to someone else. Words seemed to follow the proverbial path of going in one ear and out the other, never pausing long enough in the middle for my brain to absorb their meaning.

My inability to retain information left me concussed, which I found both disconcerting and terrifying. I felt as though I was losing my mind, until I discovered, through reading several books on post-traumatic stress disorder (PTSD), that my impairment was a normal by-product of trauma. Sadly, this temporary but serious impediment would be brought to bear in a significant way.

After Charlie died, I knew instinctively that I should not be behind the wheel of a car because I would be a danger to myself and to others. God bless my lovely niece Meghan, who stayed with me in the early weeks and drove me around town so that I could get out of the house and run errands. She told me teasingly that she was "driving Miss Daisy," and to this day, I still sign all correspondence to her "MD." Nevertheless, eight months after Charlie died, I managed to total our Subaru in a three-car accident for which I was partly to blame. Thankfully no one was injured, but knowing that the outcome could have been far worse was frightening. This fear, coupled with the necessity to purchase another vehicle, acted as great motivators. For the next year, each time I got behind the wheel, I would force myself to concentrate, perhaps overcompensating by becoming hypervigilant, but at least I was laser-focused on once again becoming the safe, confident, and competent driver I'd been before his death.

The people I needed to help me heal seemed to magically appear at just the right place, at just the right time. During that first spring, a dear friend of mine turned me on to the concept of Earthing (earthing.com). This is the process of connecting to Earth's natural energy by putting our skin in direct physical contact with soil, sand, or water. In my case, it was walking barefoot in my backyard when weather permitted. Scientifically, the earth has a mild negative charge, and over time our bodies build up a positive charge. Direct, uninterrupted surface contact with the earth, which very few of us have these days, can even out this positive charge and return the body to a neutral state. When we "ground" ourselves through surface contact with the earth, we're exchanging electrons with it, and many believe that this exchange of energy is foundational to optimal wellness: we feel better, we sleep better, and we enjoy increased energy. Then another friend taught me the benefit of just sitting on the grass for long periods of time and looking up at the sky. Both of these "grounding" techniques were extremely enjoyable and beneficial, and helped me greatly in restoring both my connection to the planet and my equilibrium.

I can't say enough about the benefits of sitting or lying on the grass and looking up! Gazing at cloud formations that morph into an animal or an angel; being awed by the aerial displays of grace, beauty, and acrobatics of a flock of birds or a pair of hawks; wondering what the people in the jets high above are thinking and doing and where they're headed; following a lone balloon as it catches the air until it's lifted out of sight; spotting the occasional satellite as it soars through the atmosphere (yes, you can see them during the day). All of these skyward marvels lifted me out of myself and gave me a deeper appreciation of the connectedness of all living things. The time I spent sitting in the grass and looking up was the time when the weight of my grief was made much lighter.

Listening to Healers

I also discovered a number of spiritual healers online and began tuning in to webcasts at Hay House, a publishing house founded by the late Louise Hay. I listened to many others, Hay, the late Dr. Wayne Dyer, Doreen Virtue, and Marianne Williamson, whose spiritual teachings and lectures are based on the 1977 book *A Course in Miracles.* I started yoga and meditation practices, which I continue today, and began an online course of study to earn a degree in metaphysical science.

One of my earlier forays into the metaphysical healing arts came by way of a search for yet another book that might help restore my wounded soul. I was guided to a title that seemed slightly outside the mainstream of books on grief and grieving that I had already come across or purchased:

Induced After Death Communication: A Miraculous Therapy for Grief and Loss by Allan L. Botkin, PsyD, and Craig Hogan, PhD. In it, Dr. Botkin explains his revolutionary discovery in 1995 of induced after-death communications, or IADC therapy for grief and trauma, that has helped countless people come to terms with their grief by allowing them the experience of private communication with their departed loved ones. The therapy employs eye movement desensitization and reprocessing, or EMDR, which is a form of psychoanalysis and is frequently used to treat people who suffer from PTSD.

I had lost Charlie only a few months before, and the idea of being able to not only see him but also talk to him one more time seemed too good to be true, but I was desperate to try. I found the one therapist in my area who had been trained and certified in Dr. Botkin's modality. I called her immediately. I was excited and hopeful, but she informed me that a candidate for the therapy needs to have grieved for at least a year before IADC could be attempted, since acute grief somehow blocks or reduces the success rate for a "communication" with the departed loved one.

I was crushed. Realizing that I was in distress and in need of more immediate relief, she referred me to Walter Zajac, a good friend of hers and a gifted psychic. To say that Walter aided me then, and continues to aid me, in my healing is an understatement. By the time the first anniversary of Charlie's death had come and gone, the compulsion to possibly see and speak to him again had waned, because I had already communicated with him through Walter!

On that first horrific night, Kathy called Logan, a wonderful friend of mine and Charlie's, to tell him what had happened. Standing right next to him was Tricia McCannon, a renowned American clairvoyant, historian, author, and teacher, and a friend of his. Tricia, who lived on the East Coast, happened to be visiting friends in Boulder, Colorado. The next day, Logan called me and said that Tricia was in Colorado for only one more day and was offering to come to my home with him that evening to help however she could and to do a group blessing to help Charlie cross over.

A number of family members and friends gathered in my home that evening. When Tricia walked in with Logan, she came right to me, hugged me, and told me some things about Charlie, his reasons for leaving the way he did—things that Logan would have been clueless about, but that I already suspected. Her loving hug and the words she said to me were remarkable, revelatory and healing. However, some of those who were gathered were very angry at Charlie for taking his own life. I wasn't yet one of those people; my anger toward him wouldn't surface until some months later. But that night, along with love and compassion, anger was hanging in the air. By the time Tricia led us through the group prayers, chants, and blessings to help Charlie transition to the other side, the anger had disappeared, and all that remained was the love and compassion and, of course, deep sadness.

To this day, everyone present still believes *her* presence was miraculous—that she happened to be standing right next to Logan when he'd received the call about Charlie— that considering her speaking engagements take her around the world, that she was in the States at all let alone in nearby

Boulder, Colorado, and finally, that she so graciously volunteered to avail herself to me and to each of us in our time of need on her last evening before her scheduled departure for home the next day—yes, it was indeed miraculous!

Tricia's visit that night was one of the first of many blessings on my journey that I will be forever grateful for. She was the light and love that temporally lifted me out of the pitch-black darkness and gave me hope that I would and could survive my grievous loss. And, not surprisingly, when I found Charlie's suicide note to me sticking out of a file drawer in our office the next day, it confirmed much of what Tricia had conveyed to me.

A month later, I sent her an email expressing my deepest gratitude for being there for me in those first hours of my anguish and despair and for setting me on the path towards healing. She sent me a beautiful reply wherein she shared with me that three days before she'd arrived in Boulder to speak at a conference, she'd lost one of her dearest girlfriends unexpectedly, who happened to reside in Boulder. I'd had no idea that while she was so graciously and selflessly tending to me in my time of profound loss, that days before, she'd experienced a profound loss of her own.

Here is an excerpt from her email:

"...Like all of those we love, she is impossible to replace. While those of us who walk between the worlds may know spiritually that there is no ending for the soul; that death is only a light-filled doorway to the higher realms, it's still hard for us who are left behind. We have emotional bodies. We have physical bodies, and we miss the ones we have shared our lives with so deeply. We miss their voices. We miss their touch. We miss tracing the lines of their face with our eyes each day, and having them sit down at the dinner table to eat with us. I get it at a deep level, and Sylvia was only my dearest friend, not my husband like Charlie was. So I know this transition is not an easy one. But it is one that Charlie wants you to make. He wants you to travel and have friends and be in the adventure and the joy of life until the day when it is your time to meet him on the Other side."

I was brought to tears by Tricia's loving and compassionate words. From her own experience with loss, she'd "known" exactly what I was feeling—how much I was missing Charlie, but she'd also "known" what I was needing and longing to hear—that he wanted me to continue to live a full and meaningful life.

* * *

So you see, from the very start, my path toward healing led me to modalities that were of a metaphysical bent. Fate and serendipity played their roles too. Whether it was a book that led me to another book, or a healer that led me to another healer, or a family member or friend who would say something or send me something that helped, synchronicity (which in the Jungian concept means meaningful coincidences) were propelling me forward.

In the ensuing days and weeks after receiving "the call," I began having a strong sense that I was being held, protected, and loved. The thought came to me that if I could but surrender to what had just happened and place my trust in God, my archangels, my guardian angels, and Charlie, I would be guided at every turn to the right people, places, and tools that would be most helpful to me in my healing. After all, the pain I was carrying was far too great to bear alone. I knew I had to release it, to hand it over to a higher authority. I knew that I'd be crushed under the weight of my grief if I didn't share it. And maybe it was because of this strong, instinctual knowing that there came into my life these series of heavenly interventions. I completely trusted that God and Universe knew best what the next step was to take. And I came to realize that nothing another person does is ever in my control. Trying to control another person's actions is as futile as trying to control the forces of nature, death being one of those forces. The only thing I had any sort of control over was how I was going to respond to this tragic event that had been placed squarely on my path.

And so I began to seek out the proverbial silver lining in the darkest of dark skies and took to heart a quote by theologian Matthew Fox: "The darkness is also a kind of revelation to divinity." I opened myself up to the possibility that maybe there were indeed blessings hiding inside those dark folds of my pain. Once I began seeking, they appeared. It is my honor and privilege to share them with you.

"They that love beyond the world cannot be separated by it. Death is but crossing the world, as friends do the seas; they live in one another still."
William Penn

3

The Blessing of Providence

"Perhaps He knew, as I did not, that the Earth was made round so that we would not see too far down the road." Isak Dinesen

FOR REASONS UNBEKNOWNST to me, I felt extremely unsettled in body and mind during the few months leading up to Charlie's passing. This unease was most pronounced when I read at night, before going to sleep. I'd find myself rubbing away on the smooth edge of a quartz rock from my garden—a rock that had somehow found its way into my hand and then onto my nightstand. I had never before employed a "worry stone" to relax me or work away my anxiety, but here I was, rubbing one furiously as I read each and every night, as though my very life depended on it. And as I read and rubbed the quartz, I would glance nervously at the phone, also on my nightstand, expecting it to ring at any moment and become the harbinger of some horrible news.

My heighted state of awareness was perplexing and exhausting. I was in a chronic state of anxiety and anticipation, waiting for some shoe to drop. I didn't share these disturbing intuitions with Charlie because I didn't want to worry him, but I did share them with my sister Priscilla. I also shared with her how, for some unfathomable reason, I could not get the opening lyrics of a Phil Collins song, "In the Air Tonight," out of my head. They played in a continuous loop. I felt something was coming, and I felt sure that it was something I had been primed for my entire life; I just didn't know what it was.

Priscilla and I shared an interest in an online spiritual website called Spirit Library and, in particular, the monthly forecasts of one of their intuitives, Sarah Varcas. Toward the end of March, we both read Sarah's April forecast. Although I can't recount the details, I remember it was disturbing, as it eerily dovetailed with and reinforced my strong feelings that something was indeed in the air and making its way toward me. I was confounded by this certainty, this awareness, this sixth sense that my life was about to shift in some significant way. At the time, our mom, whom I'm extremely close to, was closing in on 87, so I began suspecting that perhaps God and Universe were preparing me for her imminent departure. Priscilla agreed that this was the most likely explanation, although we prayed that it not come to pass.

Charlie would die at the beginning of April.

One morning, about three weeks before Charlie passed, I awoke with very specific words in my head. They had come to me as if in a dream. I knew immediately that I had to write them down, while they were still fresh in my mind. I ran into our office, where Charlie was already working at his desk, and sat down at my desk—and within ten minutes, I had written a poem that I titled "Saying Goodbye." I thought the title a bit trite and had a strong urge to change it, and I almost did, but something stopped me. I thought I'd written the poem to read to my two sisters at our upcoming gathering in Santa Fe, New Mexico, on June 14 for the 21st anniversary of our dad's passing. We were going to hold a ceremony outside of the Unity Church, just the three of us, to commemorate not only him, but all of our loved ones who had crossed over. I thought it a perfect poem to read aloud during the ceremony, and I thanked God and Universe for having gifted me with just the right words to share with them.

I told Charlie what I'd just written and why, and asked him if he'd like me to read it to him. He turned his chair around to face me, flashed that big-toothed, beautiful smile of his, and said, "Absolutely!" I did, and when I was done, he burst into tears and said, "That was so beautiful." I was a bit startled by his emotional response but also delighted that he'd found the poem so moving. I replied, "Wow! Thanks, sweetie!" I was so heartened by his reaction that I became even more excited about the prospect of sharing it with my sisters.

I knew the words that came to me that morning had originated from some magical and mystical place, which I would like to think was my soul. But the reason they were gifted to me was not what I had first believed. Not knowing what was to unfold a few weeks later, I had been given the miracle of Divine Providence. Before my journey through grief and loss was to begin, God had bestowed upon me the first of many blessings—the opportunity to say goodbye to Charlie—words from my soul to my soulmate. Upon reflection, it became very obvious why he had been moved to tears when I read him the poem. He'd known something I hadn't. He'd known that his eyes were already on another landscape and that he was already pulling away from me. He'd known that those words were my swan song to him. And, so they were.

God made the world round so we can't see what's coming, but for those few weeks leading up to my great loss, He'd flattened it out for me. He'd allowed me a glimpse of the future. Through His love, grace, and mercy, He had been preparing me for what He knew was coming. So on that fateful day, when I received "the call," and I was broken open and my heart was shattered in a million pieces; when my vessel emptied out into the Universe, and when I was plunged headlong into the deep, dark abyss of pain and suffering, even then I *knew* that God was there holding me right along with my sister, Kathy. I *knew* that He wasn't going to let this tragedy destroy me. That He was there for me to lean on. That He was there holding out his hand. That He wasn't going to let me fall so far down into the rabbit hole of grief that I'd never be able to climb back out. That He was the light through the dark night of my soul and all I needed to do was to turn it on. And so I did.

I strongly believe that I am not alone when it comes to having a sixth sense kick in before tragedy befalls us. In the case of suicide, perhaps this is more prevalent. In her book, *Facing Darkness, Finding Light: Life After Suicide*, Steffany Barton, RN, writes, "This is always the case. We are clued in, cued up to the desires and needs of our loved ones as they prepare to release the body and step into the light. Through dreams, powerful feelings, unexplained knowing, and strong urges, we receive these messages just in time. Situations coalesce and circumstances converge not by accident or happenstance, but by the alignment and synchronization of minds."

It is my belief that by saying "just in time," Barton is in no way suggesting that we blame ourselves for not decoding these clues in time to have prevented suicide. Rather, she means that the messages we may receive before loss come just in time for the survivor, to help that person get through the impending tragedy—much like my poem came just in time for me to say what I needed to say to Charlie, which brought me great peace in the aftermath of his death.

This blessing of Divine Providence, while seemingly miraculous, happens more often than you might believe. In my immediate family alone, two of four siblings also had premonitions that a loss was about to occur or had already occurred. These premonitions—or gifts of preparedness that God plants into our subconscious—can manifest in countless ways. Perhaps you had a powerful dream that clued you in. Perhaps you can reflect upon some words or a deed that you felt compelled to say or perform soon before your loved one died; some expression of love, kindness, or generosity that may have been over and above what you would normally say or do? Maybe you had an overpowering urge to give them an extra hug or kiss before they left the house that fateful day. Or you bought them something special that they'd wanted for a long time. Perhaps you took them to a place they'd longed to visit, or you decided out of the blue to prepare their favorite meal or dessert. Or like me, perhaps you experienced a deep sense of knowing—a heightened awareness and a strong premonition that something was amiss, that a great shift in life was about to occur. Divine Providence, all!

It may be a cliché, but it's also a truism: hindsight is 20/20. None of us possess the power to alter the direction our lives are meant to take. That is a fact. Looking back, it's easier to see what course corrections we might have made to spare us or our loved one from suffering. But looking forward? No one has a crystal ball that can predict future events. But sometimes, to help steel us against a great loss, God grants us a glimpse of what lies ahead—proof that He does often work in strange, mysterious, and miraculous ways. Here is my poem, a gift from God to me and then from me to my beloved.

Saying Goodbye

Saying goodbye
Without words
Too early
To be late
Moving forward
Is moving backward
All that is left
Is what is left behind
Attached
Like a colorful balloon tethered to my wrist
I hold on tightly to your joyful spirit
Which lifts my spirit upward, higher and higher
Towards you
It feels so good
Soaring to this place where our spirits connect
Pure joy
Never ending
I don't let go—I won't let go
The bubble bursts

Everything begins to unwind
Slowly at first
Then
Suddenly
Untethered
You float
Up, up, up—alone
Away from me
Me from you
Out of sight
Left behind
Learning to let go
To come to the knowing that
I never lost you
You never left me
The remains of the day are
Love and memories
The true ties that bind
Eternal and infinite
Ever-existing
Un-dying
But still
After so long
The heart aches
The longing remains
To be tethered for one more day

Karen Trench, March 2015

I was honored to read "Saying Goodbye" aloud at Charlie's Celebration of Life ceremony that took place in a field of wildflowers at 9,000 feet in the Colorado Rockies. The field was located very near our treasured log cabin that we'd sold a decade earlier—a one-of-a-kind, hand-hewn, Tolkien inspired, straight-out-of-The Shire beauty where we'd married in 1998 and in which we'd spent the best years of our lives. I and everyone in attendance that afternoon was astounded to be graced by the presence of a bull moose, rare to that location that foraged in the woods very close to the proceedings the entire time. The date was Saturday, June 27, 2015, on what would have been our seventeenth wedding anniversary.

* * *

Just as God loved and held me during my bleakest times, know that He is loving and holding you during yours. May you come to know Him as your steadfast crusader who marches shoulder to shoulder with you through your grief journey and as an eternal beacon of light who will unfailingly lead you through the darkest nights of your soul and deliver you with deep love and compassion, safely back to the dawn. Amen.

The Wisdom of Brokenness

Among The People, it is said
broken vessels are holy.
Lightening cracks mended,
bound with twine
to hold the integrity of their shapes,
they are blessed, given grain
and sacred stones to hold.
The wounds of such vessels
see, breathe, allow
inner eyes to see out,
outer eyes to see within.
Cracks, fissures,
gaping mouths of broken doorways
are passages for mothering air
to bestow her luminous light,
stir new breath,
alter the alchemy of time.
Make of my wounds gateways,
breathing and seeing;
bind up my broken shape,
fill me with still music.

Sherri Rose-Walker, 2012

41

4

The Blessing of

a Candle Flame

"As essence turns to ocean, the particles glisten. Watch how in this candle flame instant blaze all the moments you have lived." Rumi

AFTER CHARLIE DIED, I found myself taking nighttime baths. My bathtub became symbolic of returning to the womb, a nice warm place where I felt safe and protected, ensconced in a bubbly embryonic-like fluid where my salty tears could mingle with the bathwater and where I could offer up my wounded heart in a sort of ritualistic baptism of my soul. Submerging myself in the warm water made me feel more buoyant; it eased the crushing weight of grief that sat like a mountain on my chest and held my heart in a vise every waking minute of every day. My bathtub became a sacred place for me, a temporary sanctuary, a place of release and renewal.

Often, I'd light a candle and place it in front of me on one of the corners of the tub. The flickering of the flame would mesmerize me and, along with the lavender bath oil in the water, help soothe and calm me. On one particular evening, as I watched the flame, I became aware of not just the flame itself but, for the first time, the *gift* of the flame. As if looking at it with fresh eyes, I watched it as it flickered, turned, jumped, and swirled about in the dark; it became something magical and mystical as it performed its beautiful dance for me alone. I felt honored and humbled for having borne witness to it, and before I blew out the flame, I actually bowed to it in a gesture of gratitude and said, "I send your light and love out into the world." I don't know where those words came from, but now, every time I blow out a candle, my invocation is the same.

One night as I lay in my bathtub, resting my head on my bath pillow and staring at the flame, thoughts, like the flame, began to swirl around in my head. I became aware of the flame's uniqueness and singularity—and suddenly realized that with all the billions of candles that have been burned since mankind first discovered fire, and with all the billions more that will be lit, no two flames will burn in exactly the same way. I realized too that this metaphor could be applied to all living things, and I was in awe of the miracle that is creation, of our commonalities and of our individual uniqueness.

And then I thought how similar the candle and its flame are to a person and their grief. You could say that candles are universal and share universal properties. Most are made of wax or tallow, some of oil, and all have wicks. Each requires air to fan its flames. Grief is universal and shares universal properties as well: loss, sadness, shock, denial, bargaining, guilt, anger, and, ultimately, acceptance. Grief is the candle. But the flame is our grieving. And no two people have, ever will, or could dance the same dance through their grief. Our grieving is as unique to each of us as was our love for the one whose loss we grieve. Our grief is our own, and our journey through it is our own; each is as distinct and singular as the flame that so mesmerized me on that particular evening.

* * *

May your own unique and singular flame burn brightly to illuminate your path through the darkness, and may it guide you safely back to the eternal light that shines deep within you. Amen.

.

The Unbroken

There is a brokenness
out of which comes the unbroken,
a shatteredness
out of which blooms the unshatterable.
There is sorrow
beyond all grief which leads to joy
and a fragility
out of whose depths emerges strength.
There is a hollow space too vast for words
through which we pass with each loss,
out of whose darkness we are sanctioned into being.
There is a cry deeper than all sound
whose serrated edges cut the heart
as we break open
to the place inside which is unbreakable
and whole
while learning to sing.

Rashani Réa, 1991

Karen Trench

5

The Blessing of Love

*"The risk of love is loss, and the price of loss is grief—
but the pain of grief is only a shadow when compared
with the pain of never risking love."*
Hilary Stanton Zunin and Leonard Zunin

ON NOVEMBER 3, 2016, about a year and a half after Charlie
died, I received a phone call from a dear mutual friend of
ours, Rick, who informed me that his beloved wife, Vicki,
had been struck and killed by a car on her way to work that
morning. He said he was reaching out to me right away
because he knew that I would understand the gravity and
weight of his loss—how it felt to lose, in one horrible instant,
the love of your life and best friend of many years. In shock
and disbelief myself, I did the best I could to console him.

I wrote in my journal that day:

I am empathetic to Rick's pain and suffering. It is almost
too much to bear, and so, so unfathomable—when the love
of your life is simply "taken." It's the worst way to lose
someone. I think that the way she died, so traumatic, so
suddenly, and so completely has shaken me. Talk about a
seminal moment! Every truth about the fragility and
precarious nature of life slammed my brain: You never know
when you get out of bed in the morning if this will be your
last day. Life can turn on a dime. It can happen in ONE
instant. Cherish every moment. Life is such a precious gift—

don't waste one moment of it. Don't take life for granted. Live each day as though it's your last. You never know what life holds in store. Call or email everyone you love and tell them right now because you may not have the chance to do it again! Life is not promised to you. It's a gift. Live like there's no tomorrow. If you knew you were going to die tomorrow, how would you spend your last day? Neither Vicki nor Rick ever imagined that when she left her house for work this morning, that she'd never be coming home again. It does make you stop and think. As for me, I never imagined that when you left the house that day … well … that MY life would turn on a dime, but it did, just like Rick's has.

Not long before Charlie died, a couple of dear friends of ours passed, one right after the other. Upon the death of the second friend, I wrote this poem:

One falls, then another.
Faster and faster,
not two minutes
for respectful silence in between.
Suddenly over,
a truce must have been declared.
Too late.
We are alone.

Vicki's death was like being hit over the head with a cosmic two-by-four. It knocked me further from my center and caused a big shift in my soul. I felt it. It was as though I was walking between worlds. I didn't feel completely in this one, and I "felt" the next one. It was speaking to me all the time. It was a sense of not quite knowing where I belonged or how I fit in, of not knowing my place in the world. It was as though I were in a constant dream state. I was *in* the world, but not *of* the world. Nothing made sense. The shroud of my grief still felt so heavy. So many people who had made up the tapestry of my life up to that point were gone. Now, another piece on the chessboard had been removed, leaving the remaining pieces to shift yet again. One by one, the people in my lifetime who I loved and who had loved me, for a time or for all time, were leaving. With each death, a little piece of my heart died. And with each death, I began to lose my tether.

In a journal entry to Vicki, I wrote, "I will carry your ghost in my heart forever. You'll reside there with the other cherished dead with a mixture of sorrow, longing, nostalgia, gratitude, and love—but mostly love. Godspeed, and I know you're with your angels now."

My past was beginning to haunt me. My heart was growing heavy with the weight of all the ghosts it was carrying. If fate played in my favor and I was granted the gift of longevity, I reasoned that my heart would need to carry much, much more weight. This knowing guided me to write a prayer to God—a prayer that served as both an affirmation and a reminder that *everything* is always and only about love.

I was honored to read it aloud at Vicki's Celebration of Life ceremony.

"Dear God, I ask that you please help me to remember always that the weight of my sorrow is equal its weight in love. I pray that at the end of my life, my heart is overflowing with sorrow, for that will be the greatest testament that I loved and was loved deeply, richly, and well. Amen."

As we age, the weight of our sorrow only increases, for the longer we are privileged with the gift of life, the more loss, grief, and sorrow we will be asked to bear. There is no denying or escaping this hard, cold fact of life. But the contrary is also true. The longer we are privileged with the gift of life, the more love we will have the opportunity to be blessed with.

Looking upon my cumulative losses as being synonymous with love aided me greatly in shifting my focus from the pain and suffering of grieving to the joy and blessings of living! I have a garden stone hanging on my office wall with the Chinese yin-yang symbol and the word *Balance* engraved below. According to Chinese philosophy, yin is the passive female principle of the universe, characterized as sustaining and associated with earth, dark, and cold. Yang is the active male principle of the universe, characterized as creative and associated with heaven, heat, and light. The two contrary principles are actually complementary, interconnected, and interdependent, and their interaction is thought to maintain harmony in the universe and influence everything within it.

I stared at that stone frequently in my early days of grief. The symbol and what it represents brought me comfort because it's a powerful symbol of truth. Our pain and sorrow is the yin to the yang, which is love and life itself. Opposite but complementary forces coming together to teach us that life would be impossible without both the dark and the light—that each are essential components, for without one, we would never have the experience of or the appreciation of the other. For me, this "duality" equated to: the more love, the more loss; the more loss, the more love. Yin-yang. The balance of life.

I was grateful to have come to this realization, and even now I contemplate the beauty of the yin and the yang as part of my daily spiritual lessons. Life can be fickle and serendipitous. I learned this the hard way. It can end at any moment. Having had an intimate relationship with death made me appreciate even more the precious nature of life and of love. And although attempting to remain in a constant state of gratitude didn't rid me of my cumulative sorrow, it did give me greater spiritual strength to shoulder the weight of it.

For me, the grievous loss of Charlie and all previous and subsequent losses have acted as significant and powerful reminders that, for as miserable as some of my days have been, at least I'm still here! I'm vertical! I'm alive! And I get to choose, every waking moment of each day, how I want to show up in the world. I may be feeling miserable at times, but I try to turn my despair into a deeper love and appreciation of life—not just my own, but all life. And each and every loss, including the loss of cherished pets, has helped me to understand that life is a perpetual cycle of loving and then letting go, and that the experience of loving is our sole purpose and greatest blessing for having been born.

Grieving loss is the most difficult task we undertake as humans. Grief wages war and launches us into a mighty battle that we're forced to fight without regard to our readiness. Certainly, none of us is ever fully prepared for this all-out assault. The only way to escape being drafted into it is to make the supreme sacrifice—not the sacrifice of your life, but something far greater: love.

* * *

With each loss you experience, may you allow your tender heart to contain the depth of your sorrow and may you come to know that by so doing, it will be containing the depth of your love in equal measure. Allowing your heart to be filled with sorrows as they unfold is like making lifetime deposits into your bank account. Only in this case, with each loss, you're banking love, not money. I pray that before your days are done, you have a healthy balance in your love account. And I pray that you always remember that no matter what sorrows befall you, and they will, that this too shall pass, that life is beautiful and worth living, and that each and every moment you are alive is a miracle wherein you are being given the opportunity to love and be loved deeply and well. Amen.

The Guest House

This being human is a guest house.
Every morning a new arrival.

A joy, a depression, a meanness,
some momentary awareness comes
as an unexpected visitor.

Welcome and entertain them all!
Even if they're a crowd of sorrows,
who violently sweep your house
empty of its furniture,
still treat each guest honorably.
He may be clearing you out
for some new delight.

The dark thought, the shame, the malice,
meet them at the door laughing,
and invite them in.

Be grateful for whoever comes,
because each has been sent
as a guide from beyond.

Rumi

Karen Trench

6

The Blessing of Patience

"Time does restore to us our quiet joy in the spiritual presence of those we love, so that we learn to remember without pain, and to speak without choking up in tears. But all our lives we will be subject to sudden, small reminders which will bring all the old loss back overwhelmingly."
Elizabeth Watson

GRIEF IS A CONSTANT companion. Once experienced, it walks side by side with us and sticks with us like a shadow. As time goes on and our episodes of acute grief lessen, we may begin, ever so gradually, to pick up the pieces of our shattered lives and move on, with nary a word from our companion. And then, seemingly out of nowhere, our companion shows up at our doorstep, rings our doorbell, and, like an unwanted visitor, asks—no, demands—to stay with us for a period of time. When this happens, we learn that it is best not to turn our guest away but rather, as Rumi says, invite him in. Embrace him. And thank him for whatever lesson he is here to teach us.

In his book, *Grieving Mindfully*, Sameet M. Kumar uses a spiral staircase as a metaphor for the grieving process: "With each passing turn of acute grief in the spiral, no matter how many there may be, your relationship with grief and with the loved one you've lost changes. Even though there may be periods of renewal, you will also experience feelings of intense sadness and loss that may seem like setbacks. But most likely you are actually making gradual progress up the staircase of growth."

These setbacks, which are normal, most often occur when we experience a grief trigger. These triggers take many forms and are personal to each of us. They can squeeze our heart and bring us to our knees, for they are distressing reminders that our loved one is no longer with us. Some of my grief triggers were, and to some degree still are, certain songs on the radio, certain odors, certain foods, dreams, the change of seasons, rain or snow falling, holidays and all anniversaries—especially within the first year of loss—and seeing someone who resembles Charlie.

Shortly after Charlie died, I went to the grocery store and, through force of habit, I found myself at the freezer case reaching for his favorite ice cream. When I realized what I was doing, I was so overcome with emotion that I ran out of the store, leaving my cart filled with groceries in the middle of the aisle. Ice cream had triggered me! Another trigger that sent me reeling took the form of a large box of plastic kitchen garbage bags from Costco. Charlie had opened that box right before he died. Every time I pulled out one of those bags, I knew I was one bag closer to the end of the box. For some reason, this held great significance for me. It took months to get through it, but when the day finally arrived and I pulled that last bag, I found myself on my knees crying over the empty box.

They are myriad in numbers, these triggers: people, places, things, sights, sounds, smells. Some we can anticipate and steel ourselves against, like holidays, birthdays, and anniversaries; but some sneak up and stab our tender hearts. Just when we think we are anchored and on solid ground, we once again become untethered with nothing solid to hold on to. These episodes can cause us to check out emotionally and take us from normal interactions right back to curling up in a ball in a corner.

Our triggers are like the bully on the playground. We're standing there, minding our own business, feeling pretty good, when out of nowhere, the bully rushes at us and pushes us down—hard. We don't even know what hit us, but we hurt badly. We get angry and frustrated because we think that we should have been more prepared, should have seen it coming. So we stay down as long as we need to, licking our wounds until our pain subsides enough to muster the strength to stand. But the place where we find ourselves standing is miles back from the place where we were pushed. And now we need to undertake the daunting task of covering the same ground we'd already traversed, just to get back to where we were. Grief has gotten the best of us yet again.

Triggers are frustrating, and we wish they didn't have to happen. But they do. They are as inevitable as the sun rising and setting, and are a normal part of the grieving process. How we react to them may surprise not only us but also our family and friends, should they be present. We might appear perfectly calm and centered one moment, and then crumble into an emotional heap on the floor the next. So when the biggest bully, grief, knocks us down, that is precisely the time to surrender to the moment and allow your feelings, *whatever* they may be, to move through you and out of you. And there is no more perfect time than this to exercise self-love and compassion, *not* self-castigation. When a grief trigger strikes, a huge dose of patience and allowance—the knowing that "this too shall pass"—and wrapping our arms around ourselves in a big hug all aid us in a quicker return to our center.

If we can allow ourselves to go to that sweet place of surrender every time we're knocked down, we will discover that as time unfolds, we rise up faster and are stronger, more patient, and far more resilient than before. The bully may never leave the playground all together, but one day he will no longer possess the strength to bring us down. Eventually he will maintain a respectful distance.

Each of us travels up our own spiral staircase of grief. We make progress with each turn of the spiral. Then we're knocked back down a few steps. But the next time we climb, we get a little bit higher up the stairs. This is the way of grief and healing. It is important to realize, though, that there is no top step, no permanent landing that we reach and upon which we stand, finally exhale, and say, "Thank goodness that's over with. Now where's my medal?" There is no end to our grief, and no medals are awarded for enduring it. Healing is ongoing.

As author and speaker Mirabai Starr so eloquently writes, "Grief is a dynamic, ever-changing reality. There is no check-list to get through, ticking off each task as we complete it, at the end of which we are all better. It is a life-long dance, a constant opportunity to open and grow.

The trick is to approach our grief with as much awareness and compassion as we can muster." (mirabaistarr.com/rebellion/)

Our grief will be our shadow, and although it becomes less acute over time, grief will walk with us for the rest of our lives. Best to welcome it. To invite it in. To sit with it. To live with it. To embrace it. To honor it. To befriend it. For our grief is our constant reminder of our love. Without having loved so deeply, we wouldn't have a need for grief. We honor our loved ones who have left us because they have given us an opportunity to appreciate life and love and to experience personal growth.

Again, from Dr. Kumar's *Grieving Mindfully*: "Although grief stems from the end or loss of a relationship in some form, it can also be the beginning of some larger journey—a journey into the very meaning of your life. By understanding how grief unfolds, and how it blends into your life, you can view grief as a personal teacher." Grieving gives us permission to fall apart and to truly let go, and it gives us an opportunity to come together again in a more deeply loving, and spiritually enlightened way. As for me, I came to see grief as a wrecking ball: it demolished the old structure so that a new and improved one could be built!

"Walk with grief like a good friend. Listen to what he says. Sometimes the cold and dark of a cave give the opening we most want."
Rumi, from his poem, "Backpain"

* * *

May you come to know your grief not as your enemy, but as a guide who has been sent from beyond to teach you about yourself, your patience, your strength, your courage, your resilience, and your limitless capacity for love, forgiveness, and compassion. Amen.

Cracked

I'm cracked. Completely.
I fell into the furnace long enough
To decide to find my own fire and light,
And when I went all to pieces
Some surrendered to the heat
And those that were left were me
But purer: there is something of a diamond
Rushing through my core,
A full madness of restructuring.
There is no ruin here.
Unless that is your fearful name for transformation,
Which I can understand,
But when you fall flying into your own,
You'll understand:
Falling apart is full of its own reward,
However much it feels like dying, like failure
Full of the unbearable sensitivity
Of committing to this human experience.
Go deep in this fire.
There's a point where all explodes and converges,
And you find you are yourself,
Only stronger, clearer, finer.
The messiest refinement of all: Choosing to live well.
Well? Fully.

Alive to pain, to suffering, to inequality,
To joy, to birth, to creation, to love—To all,
Because when you get right down to it
Acknowledging pain only opens you more to joy.
The brilliant imperfections of love, of loving,
Can only make the world shine brighter;
It's fear that will give you half a life and convince you
You never wanted the other half anyway.

Nell Aurelia, 2014

7

The Blessing of

Transformation

"We shape clay into a pot, but it is the emptiness inside that holds whatever we want."
Tao Te Ching

LIKE YOU, I HAVE MADE DECISIONS that required a certain amount of courage—important decisions made at critical junctures that have steered the course of my life. Those were the times when I voluntarily walked to the cliff's edge, looked over, and with little or no trepidation, jumped—confident of a safe landing. When I was in control of my own choices, taking that leap of faith into the unknown tended to be easier. Plus, I had a firm understanding and appreciation of the transformative powers that resided within each and every big decision I made as my life unfolded.

But I never chose to lose Charlie. That decision was made for me, as the loss of your loved one was made for you. When I did lose him, I didn't walk fearlessly to the cliff's edge, look down into the chasm, and leap, with the assurance that I would arrive at the bottom relatively unscathed. Quite the contrary. I arrived at the edge the same way you did: Grief dragged me kicking and screaming, and then, without warning, pushed me.

As I plunged into the abyss, I tried to bargain with God. I offered up apologies, promises, and vows for past, present, and future actions if He would but spare me the agony that I knew awaited when I crash-landed. But He turned a deaf ear and a blind eye, and allowed me to sink deeper and deeper into the pit of my sorrow.

When I hit rock bottom, it wasn't pretty. Three months after my loss, I returned from the first of several trips to the East Coast to visit my mom and some of my dearest friends. But I was returning to an empty house, and I couldn't bear it. I couldn't bear the truth that Charlie would never again be home to greet me with a hug and a kiss. I ran into my garage and sequestered myself in my car to spare our two cats the trauma of hearing me wail, and now I laid across the back seat sobbing in anger and disbelief, until I exhausted myself and my tears ran dry. As I grew quiet, I began to appreciate the profound silence and the feeling of protection and safety that my car afforded me. I curled up in a fetal position and closed my eyes. As I began to doze off, I was struck with a sudden awareness. It was this: Either I could continue to fight against my new reality and remain in a state of incredulity, anger, and disbelief; or I could take my boxing gloves off and attempt to reconcile with the truth that God would not be bartering with me or sparing me my anguish. There was no escaping my plight, and the more time I spent resisting what had happened to me, the more time I would spend suffering. My choice was clear. I called a truce and surrendered to God, and it was there, in the back seat of my Subaru, where my salvation began.

Once I made the choice to align myself with Him and to place my complete faith and trust in Him, Universe, my archangels, and guardian angels—as soon as I opened my arms and my heart wide enough to "allow" them to help me with the hard work of grieving—amazing things began to happen. God began leading me to the exact people I needed to meet or see. He led me to the books I needed to read, to the words I needed to hear and write, and to the life lessons I needed to learn. It all moved me further down my path of grief and loss and aided me exponentially in my healing. The process of surrendering became inextricably linked to my transformation. I realized that if I was to become a butterfly, I would have to leave the caterpillar stage. I would have to completely give up my former life. And once I began to change, there would be no going back.

It's impossible to carry the mantle of survivor without also carrying the mantle of transformation, for they are two sides of the same coin. This holds true whether we've endured and survived a life-threatening illness or accident or the death of a loved one. And by its very nature, being a survivor all but guarantees that we are not the same person we were before our trauma. There is no way we could be, for our survival has enhanced us—it has conferred upon us gifts and blessings: greater emotional or physical strength and fortitude, resilience, and self-confidence; a deepening of faith and self-awareness; a deeper love and compassion for self and others; and a far greater love and appreciation of life than we ever had before. To quote psychologist Susan Powers, PhD, from her book *Ruthless Grieving,* "Grief takes a hold of you and shakes all the "not you" from you, and what is left is so much closer to who you really are. So you shouldn't want to be the same, and you are not, but in so many ways you have a chance to become more whole and more deeply yourself."

Not only did Charlie's death transform me in all the ways I outlined above, but his passing also gave me the impetus and the courage to resurrect my writing career. I take pride too in my ability to manage my home and finances, two challenges that when confronted, many widows find daunting. However, the most meaningful and profound transformation has been the deepening of my spirituality and spiritual practice. Beginning in the weeks preceding his death and continuing beyond it, I believed strongly that I was being guided by God and held in the arms of angels. Knowing that I still am and will always be guided is the greatest source of peace and comfort and the greatest blessing that has been bestowed upon me since losing Charlie. Grief transformed me into a spiritual seeker, and I look forward to spending the rest of my life discovering!

Whether we arrive at the cliff's edge on our own terms or on God's, the outcome is the same: transformation! Perhaps the likelihood that we'll crash and burn is far greater when we are pushed over the edge, versus going there willingly, but we must take heart. We can learn from and be uplifted by the legend of *The Phoenix*, the bird who, after living five hundred years, burned itself on a funeral pyre only to rise again in a blaze of glory. We too can rise from the ashes of our pain and suffering and be completely reborn and made anew. Death. Rebirth. Transformation.

"Glory to the phoenix for teaching us that ashes are not an end point, but a bed for consummating that which is destined to be reborn."
Jamie K. Reaser

The ritual of grieving is hard work. Its long arms wrap around us and squeeze our hearts until we can barely breathe. It wrests control and takes us to the deepest depths of despair. We experience many days, weeks, months, and sometimes years in abject anguish, exhaustion, and confusion; feeling out of control, untethered, and ungrounded; and being angry over having been left behind to try and rediscover some scrap of meaning, some purpose again in our lives. Our sorrow is beyond measure. We may find ourselves at times with our fists raised high, shaking them furiously and shouting, "Why me?" or "I can't do this! I don't want to do this!" We beseech God to please, please, please lift the grueling weight of sorrow off our shoulders NOW! We grow impatient with our grief.

It is in those moments of absolute despair that most of us believe we lack the strength to keep walking through hell. We believe that no matter how hard or how fast we walk, there will be no end to it—that we'll never make it to the light at the end of our long, winding, pitch-black tunnel. In fact, we begin to doubt the light's very existence. We're completely wrung out. We want desperately to give up the fight and admit defeat. We walk around aimlessly, in circles, lost wayfarers without a compass to guide us back home. We're completely on our own.

What's worse is that when we do eventually find our way, we discover that what we're returning to in no way looks familiar. It's like waking up in a *Twilight Zone* episode. We experience a complete shift in our reality. Our loss and grief transform us entirely. This is not something we are going to "get over." We will claw our way back to being whole again, to living with the loss, but we will never be the same. If there were guideposts on our journey through grief, then this place of "knowing"—that we and the life we knew before have been inexorably changed—would be the first place we arrived at on our way toward deeper understanding and healing.

As time passes, we come to realize that our healing demands much of us. It demands that we release and surrender layers of our old selves and our old lives to accommodate the many changes in our new lives, whether we like some of those changes or not. And as painful and difficult as this "letting-go-of" can be, we must remember that no birth is without pain and that eventually, our suffering will lead us to a point on our path when we need to decide who we will *become* because of what we have gone through—*in spite of* what we have gone through. It is here at this crossroads where we will need to choose what we wish to pursue and how we wish to spend the rest of our lives. If we can release the life we knew and courageously embrace the unknown life that awaits, imagine the endless ways we can begin to replenish our empty vessel—body, mind, and spirit! If we tend to things at our deepest levels, our grief becomes integrated into our very being.

"Yet, in fact, it's when we face the darkness squarely in the eye—in ourselves and in the world—that we begin at last to see the light. And that is the alchemy of personal transformation. In the midst of the deepest, darkest night, when we feel more humbled by life, the faint shadow of our wings begins to appear."
Marianne Williamson, The Gift of Change

* * *

May you emerge from the chrysalis of your grief a beautiful butterfly, and may you stand in awe at yourself and the metamorphosis you endured to get there. Amen.

"In the end, only three things matter:
How much you loved, how gently you lived, and how
gracefully you let go of things not meant for you."
Buddha

8

The Blessing of Surrender

"A tree that is unbending is easily broken."
Lao Tzu

I WROTE THE FOLLOWING in my journal the first autumn after Charlie died:

It is autumn; the season of change. As I look at the leaves on my neighbors' tree, now bright yellow, I am in wonder of them. They are, each one, unique. They are the leaves of this year, of this season. The leaves that clung to the very same branches in seasons past are long gone. Soon, these leaves too will be long gone. They budded in the springtime and flashed their greenery proudly all summer long. As the season stretched and the days became shorter, their color began to fade until they morphed into the color of the sun. Soon, a strong wind or even a slight breeze will unhinge each from the branch that has been its home for a season. They will not cling to the branch. They will let go. Like fearless paratroopers, each will sail through the air without question, without care or concern as to how they will land, where they will land, or what will happen to them once they land. Many will end up in garbage bags to be hauled away. Many will be blown great distances by the wind. Still more will be washed down the curbside drains and carried away by water. But they will not resist the garbage bags, the wind, or the water. They will just go. And the tree? Well, she will remain grounded. Deeply rooted in the present. She will offer herself up and surrender layer upon layer of her bejeweled finery until inevitably, she will be completely disrobed. And as the cold winds of winter blow through her naked branches, she will not stand rigid against the winds, because that would surely break her. Instead, she will soften her limbs and welcome them. She will allow them to rush through and around her. She will bend and sway and dance with the wind. She will allow even the harshest of them to have their way with her, and she will surrender to whatever fate blows her way. If it is time for her to be uprooted or to die, she will not resist; she will simply allow herself to go. For everything in its time must go. If she survives the winter, her roots will grow deeper still, she will re-manifest herself and will once again be adorned in the springtime with another beautiful outfit that will be a feast for my grateful eyes. Her miraculous cycle of life will continue. She will mature and grow more beautiful with each passing season.

Please dear God, I pray that I may live my life like the trees and the leaves. That I may remain rooted in the present moment. That I may live in a constant state of sweet surrender. That I may, without resistance, allow what is to be. Amen.

Charlie passed in early spring: April 6, the day after Easter, 2015. We'd always been avid walkers, he and I. Now I was walking solo, in every way. As challenging as it was to take "our" walk alone, I found that being outdoors and in nature—two things that Charlie and I cherished—brought him closer to me. I found comfort, cold as it was, when my eyes rested on something that his eyes had once looked upon; it made me feel like he was inside of me looking out at the rising landscape through my eyes. May and early June were frigid and wet, unusual even for Colorado. The trees and bushes and flowers, many budding or in bloom, took a hit when we got slammed with a late spring snowstorm. Many lost all their buds and flowers; some lost entire limbs, and a few were killed outright. Yet, it took only two weeks for those battered trees and bushes to transform into healthy, blossoming objects of beauty.

I have always been amazed at the resiliency of nature and the change of seasons, each holding the promise of rebirth, and I couldn't help but draw a comparison. They had endured the worst that had befallen them with complete equanimity. They had survived and were now thriving. I was nowhere near this resilient. I was still feeling battered and torn. But those trees and bushes and the blossoming of spring gave me hope and a vision. If I could simply give myself over entirely to God and Holy Spirit and to allow all to unfold as it should, to trust that all was unfolding as it should, to surrender to all that unfolded and to accept all that unfolded, then perhaps I too could one day spring back to life—maybe feeling stronger, more courageous, and more beautiful because of, not in spite of, what I'd endured.

One of the most upsetting and difficult tasks many of us face upon the death of a loved one is to begin relinquishing that person's possessions. For some, this letting-go-of begins almost immediately, as was the case for me. After all, the reality of what happened had hit me like a Mack truck. I was alone. Charlie was never coming home again. I was going to have to find some way to carry on without him. For me, looking at all of his things just made my heart break that much more. They were all horrible reminders of his aliveness. His possessions haunted me, all of them rendered completely meaningless. Leftover remnants of a ghost. Charlie would never read one of his books, use one of his tools or any of his toiletries, or wear one article of his clothing again. Someone else would benefit from most of these things.

I saved some cherished items for myself and chose others to be passed along to family and friends as mementoes. The rest was given away. A mere three weeks after he died, on April 26, I wrote in my journal:

It tore my heart out to do it, sweetie, but today, I cleaned out the toiletries from your bathroom and the linen closet. Just the beginning of an unimaginable task—getting rid of pieces of you, one by one by one. It's heartbreaking. As I was performing this gut-wrenching task, our neighborhood was bustling with folks doing yard work; living life as usual. I was surrounded by noise—chainsaws buzzing, leaf-blowers blasting—you would have hated that ... and then me, suddenly needing air and escaping onto our deck. I found the one private spot away from everyone's view, and wept uncontrollably and wondered what our neighbors would think if they knew that in our house, a newly minted widow was beginning the excruciating task of removing remnants of you and of our—my—past life. I was so angry at their oblivion, but so, so envious of it at the same time. It was all so surreal!!

These rites of passage through my grief—the physical, emotional, and material release of Charlie—continued.

On May 20, I wrote:

Woke up with yet another poem in my head. Had to write it down as soon as I got up:

I wake each day without a care
Because you're not there
To share time and space
Without a trace
Each moment on the clock's face
Tick, tick, ticks by
Within each, an eternity
Billions of ticks left to go
Timeless eternities without you.

May 22:

Sweetie, it's been raining or snowing and fairly cold since you passed. I think the earth is in mourning for you just as I am. This morning, I decided to begin the "book" process and removed and boxed up most of your books from the bedroom bookcase. It is an EXCRUCIATING task ... removing you a little at a time ... one book at a time. You used old play or concert tickets as bookmarks, which brought back such sweet but haunting memories; sometimes old business cards ... those sad reminders of just how many iterations of careers you (and you and I) had attempted over the many years. It all seems so exhausting looking back—no wonder you got so tired. I have read your last letter to me countless times. When I read it again this morning, I was struck to the core because I just can't believe how much you were holding in over the years and not sharing; not with me or anyone! ... I am so sorry for you that you felt your only option to have some peace was to leave me. But if you had no more joy and no more to offer to or of yourself—and ostensibly to me—well, it's just so heart shattering!!

June 17:

When I was still struggling with how to empty our office, I was looking for signs that Charlie was still with me:

Was that you yesterday morning beeping the smoke alarm in the office ever so gently? I was in a state at that moment, wailing and sobbing. Was that you telling me that you're still with me? And was that balloon I saw way, way up in the sky on a walk last week—was that you, too? I think it was. Oh, sweetie, you have no idea. There are no words. How am I going to live the rest of my life without you by my side? I am so lonely—so missing you! My soul aches for you! Help me as much as you can wherever you are. I beg you! Help me. Guide me. Give me advice. Stay with me. Let me feel you. I can't bear this life without you. I am struggling. I want to give up. Every moment is anguish. Give me strength to keep going. I PLEAD with you! I BESEECH you! My life as I knew it with you is gone. That's what it feels like. I've never known such deep sorrow. Now I'm living in it every moment of every day. I feel so alone. I am so scared. How am I going to find my way back into the world without you? It seems an impossibility right now. Please, please keep letting me know you're with me. My heart and soul are shattered.

July 10:

Today is the day I begin to really release you into the ethers. Steve is sending Terry and Max over to buy your best tools. My heart is so heavy, sweetie. You loved your tools. You took such pride in them and used them over the many years to build things ... for me ... for us. You used them to make our lives easier and better. If I thought my heart couldn't ache any more than it already does, I was wrong. Please give me strength. Be by my side and let me know that I'm only doing what needs to be done. I am in anguish! I couldn't love you or miss you more if I tried.

This painful letting-go-of continued.

July 28:

We were networked for twenty-three years; glued at the hip. Today, some guy from Geek Squad is coming over to detach our computer network, as you suggested in the letter you left me. This is SO hard for me; so many emotions tied up. You were glued to your computer for years and years; we were attached—sharing an office almost always. Time to separate; another case of me having to let you go; of trying to make room for a new life; alone, without you. It's all so horribly, excruciatingly painful! I never knew the depths that pain and agony can reach. It seems almost inhuman; primordial ... sheer ANGUISH!! Please help me to stay strong, sweetie. I need you now more than ever!

August 6:

It's been 122 days since I last saw you, sweetie. Four months; a quarter of a year ... feels like 4 years. I had a very rough day. Kathy, Mom, and Priscilla pulled me through. Knowing that we spent over 8,000 days together ... and realizing I may well have to endure that many more without you ... well, it is simply inconceivable to me! How will I ever survive the rest of my days without you?!! This from Priscilla: 'Four months feels like four years; four minutes, forty times four to infinity where only love is real.' Omar is coming tomorrow, sweetie, to take your desk and your file drawers. This morning, I literally lay prone on your desktop, now cleared of all of your things, and sobbed; wretched, jagged, soulful sobs that came from somewhere further than the deepest part of my being; so much blood, sweat, and tears you had shed over that desktop over so many years. Now it is my turn to shed my tears, for you and for me, for all you accomplished while working at your desk, providing us with so much, laboring and toiling away ... to what end, though? To what end? To such a tragic, desperate end? Tomorrow there will be a physical void across the room, a place you used to occupy in such a big way. How will I fill it? How will I bear the truth that I will never again be able to turn my chair around to look at you sitting at your desk, to ask you a question, to share something with you, to just gaze upon you, or to simply say, 'I love you, sweetie.' How will I get through letting-go-of ... letting go of you one piece at a time? My heart aches and breaks for you; and for me; for us ... for what was. I'm trying to let go sweetie ... but I'm not ready yet. Please stay with me for a while longer. I'm just not ready yet.

August 8:

I released the rest of your clothes to RJ, sweetie. He was so thrilled ... like a kid in a candy shop. I know this would have pleased you to no end! All of your beautiful clothing went to an old buddy and someone who truly appreciated it so much! It was the perfect unfolding for such a VERY difficult letting-go-of!!

August 15, feeling so lonely:

On my walk today, I saw a lone duck swimming in the pond. She and I were the same at that moment. But when I was walking back home, another duck, her mate, had appeared, and suddenly I was jealous of that female duck! The entire time I was walking, I thought that I would feel a tap on my shoulder, or that I'd literally run into you ... I felt it so strongly. I noticed that some leaves are showing the slightest hint of yellow ... the season is turning ... spring is when you left me ... it gave way to summer ... now summer will give way to autumn and on and on, forever ... everything continues to fall away ... everything is impermanent—everything shall pass. What never passes, what will never die or fade, is my love for you. God, how I miss you!

March 2016:

I realized on my walk in the snow this morning that it's harder forging new tracks than retracing the old ones.

April 1, 2016, days before the first anniversary of his death:

Five more days before I take my cliff dive ... over the edge and into the deep end. I'm hoping that when I surface I can finally let out the breath that I feel I've been holding for over a year. You took your own cliff dive that day a year ago, sweetie. Now I know that you were heading towards that cliff for a number of years ... on April 6, 2015, you jumped. You never resurfaced. You never got to breathe again. Will I really ever breathe again? Or will it feel like I'm hooked up to a respirator? My chest might move up and down, but will I really be living? Will I really be able to breathe on my own ever again? You were the one who breathed life into my very core. You were the life force that kept me moving forward. When you stopped breathing, I stopped. How will I ever learn to do that by myself? Our life together was like an impressionist painting; everything was so real, so vivid, so colorful and alive. So easy to make sense of. There was always a sense of peace and beauty and love in our life together. Now, I feel like I'm living in a Picasso painting; it sort of looks like something, but I can't quite discern what it is. It's misshapen, bent, crooked—makes no sense at all; everything jumbled together to look like something but not quite. That's my life now, without you. I suppose at times it's like a Dali painting, too—so surreal—nothing like the painting you and I created together. Now it's up to only me to create a painting that makes some sense to me again, that will project beauty again, just a different sort of beauty. My painting will never be ours, the one that we created. It can't be. It will be mine and mine alone. But how do I even begin? How do I begin picking the paint colors? What brush will I know to use? What texture will my painting have? What hue will radiate from the canvas? I am the creator, the artist; I will create my new life without you. You left me no choice. If it's going to be, it's up to me.

On April 6, 2016, the one-year anniversary of his death, I first wrote down part of a poem by Pablo Neruda titled "The Dead Woman" (from the film *Truly Madly Deeply*). The poem speaks of a man, perhaps the author himself, imagining the unimaginable death of his beloved and saying that if she has died, that his feet would want to walk to where she is sleeping, but that instead, "I shall stay alive." Still lamenting Charlie's death, Neruda's poem resonated deeply with me. I wished that somehow I could walk to wherever Charlie was. But he was gone and I was here—still alive and still alone.

Then I wrote down my own poem—written for me, to me:

Rest easy and be not afraid. Instead, know that time will take care of itself.
Instead, trust that your future is unfolding exactly as it should be.
Instead, embrace and live in this very moment ...
And in this one.
And in this one.
And in this one.
And in this one.
And in this one.

Upon reflection, I was struck by the words I had used in my earlier journal entries, some of which I repeated over and over to describe my emotional state at the time—*excruciating, anguish, agony, gut-wrenching, inhuman, painful, inconceivable, surreal, heart shattering, exhausting*—as compared to the entries I wrote as I approached the one-year anniversary. The later ones reveal how much more "reconciled" I had become; rather than looking back with longing and regret on the road I'd already traveled, I was beginning to set my gaze upon the road before me.

Although I was *beginning* to assimilate my loss and to surrender to my new life without Charlie, after a year and a half I was still struggling mightily to find my sense of self and my place in the world.

October 9, 2016:

I feel as though I'm waiting for something to be over that's never going to be over. I am in a state of limbo, a feeling of being untethered—or maybe of feeling I'm half in this world and half in the next; definitely not all in this one! Sort of like I'm living in a fishbowl. The world outside takes on a surreal and dreamlike quality; everything is distorted, unreal ... blurred and fuzzy from my viewpoint. My little world inside the fishbowl is the only world that feels right; where I feel safe, protected and loved. But I know I can't live in a fishbowl forever. I have to find my way back into the world, as strange and scary as it appears to be. And I have to be okay with it when I finally do. Therein lies the greatest challenge. I suppose the opposite could be true. Everything beyond the glass of my fishbowl is what's really clear and real, and it's what's in the fishbowl that is unclear and unreal. Perspective. No matter, I must muster the courage to leave the protection and security of my little bowl to find my place in the world again, no matter how hard that might be to accomplish by myself ... without you, my love ... without any man, maybe forever. If not forever, then at least for a while. I have to find my own way now, through the darkness, the fear, the insecurity of not knowing what lies around the next bend. I have to discover my own powers, my own strengths, and how I can be of the highest good to myself, my world, and my God for the remainder of my life. Please help me, my love. Please continue to sit by my side and to guide me. Help me to overcome my fears and bring me to that place of pure love and light and of KNOWING. I want to make you proud of me.

By early January 2017, twenty-one months after he died, I wrote a journal entry that was surprising even to myself. I beseeched both Charlie and Grief to release me from their grasp.

I don't want to be your kite. Not unless when I'm in the prime of my upward arc, you let go of my string. I don't want restraints. I don't want to be controlled or manipulated by you to go this way and that. I don't want to be weighed down by the heaviness of the earth's pull; the gravity chokes me. I am meant now to soar free, to let the Tiger Wind grab my Kite Tail and lift me as high as it wants to carry me; to a place where the air is lighter; where I can breathe; where it has its way with me and takes me wherever it chooses. Beyond all confines, all boundaries; where no one tugs at me, to try to keep me in my place, to give me only so much space to grow, only to then rein me in so that I can fly only so high. This is my dance, my journey. Let me discover now how high I can truly fly. Who knows? Perhaps I'll fly higher than all of my imagined fears, my limitations, and beyond! But I'll never know unless you first let go of my string. Release me so that I can discover just how high I can fly!

It was then, almost two years into my grief journey, that I instinctively knew I had reached a significant place on my path that was telling me I was slowly, but surely, integrating the loss of Charlie into my being. That now, more than ever before, Charlie was literally a part of me; that there was no separation really, because love doesn't "go" anywhere. He was safe and whole and carried deep within my heart, then and always. This was a great revelation to me. The process of surrendering his belongings on the physical plane earlier in my journey didn't mean he was gone. Instead it had brought me closer on a spiritual plane to that final stage of grief: acceptance. God had graced me with the gift of knowing that I was, at least, heading in the right direction. I knew that my life force was beginning to spring forth again and was calling me toward growth. And I knew that I had become both a participant and a witness to the healing of my heart.

Beginning the overwhelming task of relinquishing the physical belongings of your loved one requires great courage and determination. You must be resolute. You must steel yourself against the onslaught of grief that comes with this step. Surrendering the material items that exemplified the life of the one you lost and the loss of the life you shared is one of the most excruciating actions you will face. It is one of many signposts you will arrive at along the grief journey. Getting there may take you weeks, months, or even years. No matter.

I can't overemphasize this enough: Your journey is your own, and YOU get to decide how to take it. There is NO right or wrong way! But when you do arrive here—at this signpost of "surrender"—you need to give yourself a big pat on the back. For the odds are great that when you are ready to move on in your journey, you will leave knowing something vital: that the love you and your loved one shared never resided in the realm of the material, but in the eternal realm of the spiritual—within your heart and within the memories of your heart. Thus you will also know that there truly *is* a life awaiting you beyond the acuteness of your grief, even if you can't imagine yet what that will look like without the presence of your loved one.

Lastly, you will know that you are beginning to become reconciled to your grief, and are slowly assimilating and integrating the loss of your loved one into your very being.

"We are far stronger than our pain. It can come in waves, move through us, spice up our life, but suffering, that happens when we fight it, shut the door and hold off, shouting, 'No. You should not be here.' There is no should. There only is. And when you accept that, letting the emotion rise, the feeling crest and crash, say to it, 'it's ok. I accept you.' Even say to it, 'I love you.' There is power there. There is freedom."
Kamal Ravikant, Live Your Truth

The vastness of our grief is like an ocean, and we are like a piece of sea glass that has been thrown into the deep end. We let the waves wash over us. We allow them to tumble us to and fro, to annihilate us over and over and over again. We learn to ride the current. We learn how to surrender to the tidal wave of our sorrow and to trust that with each wave, we are being carried closer and closer to shore. And that when we do finally come to rest in the sand, we arrive purified and transformed. This is the only way to smooth the rough edges of our grief. We must surrender to it. And unlike in wartime battles, where surrendering means giving up and waving the white flag in defeat, surrendering in our battle with grief means giving ourselves over to the process, with trust and faith that in time, this too shall pass.

> *"Like a sandcastle, all is temporary.*
> *Build it, tend it, enjoy it.*
> *And when the time comes,*
> *let it go."*
> *Jack Kornfield*

***

May you live your life like the trees and the leaves; rooted in the present moment, living in a constant state of sweet surrender, and like them, without resisting, allow what is to be. Amen.

Picking Up the Pieces

It's so hard to pick up the pieces
after a fall so far.
How does one let go of
the hopes and dreams
you had only yesterday?

And yet life does go on.
One foot in front of the other.
One moment at a time.
One day at a time.

Look to those who love you, Child.
They will lift you up
much as you have done
for them in the past.

Look to your heart
that will begin to find another path.
That will begin to
find new hopes and dreams
worth living for.

And soon there will be a new you.
It might not be tomorrow.

101

It might not be for a while.
But it will happen.

For life has a way of
getting us through these times.
With love from others,
with love for ourselves,
we pick up the pieces and find our way home.

Elizabeth Adams, 2016

9

The Blessing of Others

Karen Trench

"True love and faith arrive when it's most dark. In the dark, there is a special kind of beauty. In a dark time, your eyes can see your true friends by the light of their lamps."
Jack Kornfield, *A Lamp in the Darkness*

AT THE ONE-YEAR ANNIVERSARY of Charlie's death, I sent an email to all my friends and family and included a link to a *YouTube* music video of *My Heart Will Go On* by Celine Dion, from the movie *Titanic*. The email read:

Thank you all for every act of kindness and compassion you have bestowed upon me during the last year, and they came to me in many, many forms! You let me lean on you and shouldered me as I shared my grief and my burdens. You showered me with unconditional love and helped sustain me and to keep me strong. Because of you, I am ready to move forward with optimism and hope into my new life. I will NEVER forget you or the beautiful memories Charlie and I shared with each of you over the many years. You, those cherished memories, and my beloved Charlie will live forever within my full and grateful heart. It is because of YOUR open, loving, beautiful hearts that MY heart WILL go on. My friends and family are indeed the people through whom God loves me. I remain forever yours in love, light, gratitude, and friendship.

Although no one could grieve for me, they certainly could and did grieve with me. That became evident the night that Charlie died, and on subsequent days and nights when family and friends gathered at my home to be with me, to cry with me, and to share and process our collective and profound loss. The love and compassion they showed me always, but especially at the beginning of my journey through the pitch-black darkness, is something I will never forget and will cherish until my dying day.

That first night, my sister Priscilla was traveling with her then-boyfriend, James, from Kansas City, Missouri, where they'd spent Easter weekend with his family, back to their home in Santa Fe, New Mexico. My sister Kathy's call had intercepted them at the halfway point, and they immediately headed to Denver. By the time they arrived, close to midnight, the shock of what had happened a mere six hours earlier had set in for me. Prior to their arrival, I just sat in one spot on my couch in a state of suspended animation. I sensed people moving about, but I wasn't "seeing" them. I recall hearing people speaking, and I even think that at times, they were speaking directly to me, but I had no clue as to what they were saying, and if I did respond to anyone, I have no recollection of it. And I don't recall crying. For that period of time, in that altered state, I was both deaf and mute.

The first clear memory I have of moving and speaking was to Priscilla. I stood to greet her and James at the door. She rushed into my arms and hugged me tightly—I think she was crying.

We sat holding each other for what seemed a long time, and at some point, the idea that a hot bath might help soothe me must have been discussed, as I vaguely remember Priscilla leading me up my stairs and into my bathroom. My legs were all wobbly like jelly, and I could hardly stand, let alone balance myself. She held me close, and I clung to the railing tightly as I climbed, needing all the support I could get. She carefully sat me down on the toilet seat cover while she ran a hot bath, and then helped me undress. She grabbed both of my hands and steadied me as I climbed into the bathtub, where she guided me first into a seated position and then gently onto my back. I remember the scent of lavender bath oil and of her cradling the back of my head with one hand, much like one bathes an infant, while with the other she tenderly and lovingly washed me.

That night, Priscilla had anointed me—not only in the traditional sense, with lavender bath oil, but with the deepest love, compassion, and grace that one human being can confer upon another. This shared intimacy between two sisters—on a physical, emotional, and spiritual plane—was deeper and richer than anything we had ever shared. She was my big sister, and I'd known her all my life. She was there first. What she bestowed upon me was the blessing of a ceremonial ritual that I can only describe now as near holy, a sacrament.

My temple inside was empty. A simple bath was elevated to an ablution, a sacred cleansing and purification of the outside of my temple, and served to symbolically prepare me for my rite of passage through the darkness. But her loving act also served to reignite the pilot light *inside* that would one day burn bright again. Just as God breathes life into Adam in the famous Michelangelo fresco *The Creation of Adam*, so had Priscilla breathed life back into my body as I lay there that night in my bathtub, lifeless, on my back in total surrender.

107

After she dried and dressed me, she led me back downstairs and onto the couch, where she laid me across her lap. She cloaked me in her loving arms and rocked me gently as I whimpered like a wounded animal. And that's where we remained for that entire sleepless first night.

Very recently, Priscilla shared a memory about that evening in an email: "The moment I entered your home on that fateful night nearly four years ago, I saw a wounded bird who fell out of her tree—fragile, broken, vulnerable; all I could think to do was wrap my wings around you and hold you, trying to make you feel safe, protected, warm, held. It was as if I believed somehow I could infuse you with my very lifeblood that first night and those first painful days and weeks."

As Kathy and I had been brought closer that day because of what we'd shared, so too had Priscilla and I. My sisters are such blessings to me!

In her book *Falling Out of Grace,* Sobonfu E. Somé writes, "In the village, there is the belief that when anyone passes, no matter what their place in the community, something valuable to everyone is lost. Every death affects every person. Everyone grieves together. One thing that is often overlooked in the west is the importance of collective grief. When a death is not grieved by the whole community together, it leaves the individuals who were closest to the deceased shattered and alone. They end up without a path back to the life of the group."

Each life is a stone cast in a pond. There is no way to predict the ripple effect of that one life lived and lost. The loss of Charlie impacted many lives, not just mine. While I had lost my husband, it did not escape me that everyone gathered around me in those early days was mourning the loss of a beloved friend, father, father-in-law, grandfather, brother, brother-in-law, or son-in-law.

There is an old Irish proverb that says, "It is in the shelter of each other that the people live." In times of mourning, we seek solace in the arms of others, in their kind words, deeds, and gestures. We gather round each other to grieve collectively and to shepherd each other through our communal loss. We lean in and allow our hearts to open and receive all the love and support that is there for us. We allow ourselves to be held, to be carried, to be nurtured and to be vulnerable—and in turn, if we're able, we do the same for those who may be grieving right along with us. We learn to hold ourselves and each other—our hearts, our pain, and our suffering—in great compassion.

While your journey through grief and loss is your own, you never need to walk it alone, not unless you choose to. And as I discuss in the next chapter, "The Blessings of Silence, Nature, and Wisdom," there is a time to embrace solitude to further aid you in your healing. I might add that if the consolation and support of family or friends is not immediately available to you, fear not! A quick online search will guide you to a number of grief support groups that are available in your community, as well as grief counselors or therapists who could meet with you on an individual basis. Or if you prefer, there are numerous grief and loss websites that are there to aid and comfort those of us who are grieving; many tailored to a specific loss such as the loss of a spouse/partner, a child, a parent, a sibling, friend or pet.

My own online search guided me to two support groups specifically for suicide survivors, and I briefly joined one.

Although it was emotionally challenging for me, I did find that sharing my feelings with people who had lost a loved one in the same tragic manner was extremely healing. Hearing their stories and sharing mine helped remove some of the shame and stigma that suicide survivors often face. They made me feel safe, included, and less alone. As I healed, I felt strong enough to leave group support for individual therapy. However, both forms of support aided me greatly in moving my "ball of grief" further down the field.

Bottom line, you *never* need to shoulder the weight of your grief by yourself. There are many people available to you who want nothing more than to help you carry your load. All you need do is to let them.

As I mentioned above, there is a stigma that surrounds suicide and, sadly, suicide survivors. But what I have come to learn is that there is a societal stigma surrounding death in general. When someone we know has died, it reminds us of our own mortality. We become uncomfortable because their death is a reminder that our own death and the death of our loved ones is imminent, and we can't bear the thought of either occurrence. We're terrified to look death square in the face until the death of a close friend or family member holds a mirror up to us and forces us to take a good look. And in our society, people don't openly discuss death.

All of this can lead to some pretty awkward behavior when we find ourselves in the presence of someone who has lost a loved one. We may say something perfectly acceptable but trite or inadequate such as, "I'm so sorry for your loss." Or we say something completely inappropriate—or worse, we avert our gaze all together and remain speechless, acting as though nothing has happened. Two days after Charlie died, a well-intentioned girlfriend called me and actually asked me out to lunch! I could barely move from my chair because the weight of my grief was so heavy that the mere idea of meeting a girlfriend for lunch seemed not only ludicrous, but insulting.

Being on the receiving end of people's condolences, I encountered a myriad of responses and reactions. It didn't help that I vowed from day one that no matter what, I was never going to lie to anyone who asked me how my husband had perished. Ever. And I have kept my vow. After all, it's my truth. But admitting that he committed suicide has made for some *very* uncomfortable and awkward moments—not for me so much as for the person who asked.

But here is what I've come to know. In our time of bereavement, people's words or deeds can either make us feel extremely comforted or can unintentionally hurt us. And if someone unintentionally hurts us or if we feel slighted in some way, instead of feeling angry, disappointed, or disrespected, we should try to show them a measure of compassion and mercy. After all, who among us has not been on the giving end of extending condolences? And who among us hasn't felt somewhat awkward or at a loss for just the right words during those challenging times? Forgiving ourselves our own possible trespasses allows us to be more forgiving of those who may unintentionally trespass against us during our time of loss. Each of us is only human after all, complete with fears, foibles, and insecurities that can manifest at times in the worst ways—but most especially under the specter of death.

* * *

May you never walk alone on your journey through grief, and may you seek comfort in the arms of angels, whose faces are those of your family, your friends, your healers, your community, and your community of faith. Amen.

Complexities of Solitude

Deep in the beautiful dimension
The Book of Truth opens.
Rumi

Music threads through still, fragrant air
in golden rooms sheltering
memory, dream, reverie,
interlace of shadow and light.
Mourning, too, weaves through it;
grief spreads her dark skirts
rich with subtle gifts.
Roses open intricate petals
etched in runic secrets
while birds murmur
in their arcane and musical tongue.
Soul breathes, expands, spreads her wings in quiet light.
The Book of Wisdom opens.

Sherri Rose-Walker, 2017

10

The Blessings of Silence, Nature, and Wisdom

"Be still and know that I am God. Be still and know that I am. Be still and know. Be still. Be."
Psalm 46:10

WHILE REACHING OUT TO OTHERS when we are grieving is a vital component of our overall emotional well-being and healing, so too is spending time alone. Our grief is calling us, entreating us to turn inward so that we can hear this inner voice of Divine Guidance. But in order to hear this inner voice with its words of strength, insight, and courage, we must learn to be still, we must enter the silence, and we must listen.

Being still and entering the silence is easier said than done. There is an entire world out there begging for our attention. Every distraction under the sun, even under our own roof, can tempt us off the path. This is not to suggest that we should shut life out entirely while we grieve. After all, one of the most significant "rewards" for allowing ourselves to grieve our loss is the gateway that it opens to a renewed appreciation for living, for all of life, and for the reclamation and restoration of life's purpose and meaning. So whether it be watching television, going to a movie, visiting a neighbor, or going away for the weekend with family or friends, we welcome these distractions. Each is a beautiful reminder that life goes on after loss and is calling us forward toward growth. Engaging in activities outside of ourselves temporarily lifts us up and out of our sorrow, and that's a good thing.

What we must be mindful of, however, is the temptation to tamp down our pain and suffering by evading it, avoiding it, or keeping ourselves overly busy. If we give in to that temptation, we will be missing one of the most beautiful gifts and blessings that grieving bestows upon us: the blessing of wisdom.

Before Charlie died, it was just the two of us living out the rest of our lives together. When he died, it became just me, trying to figure how I was going to live another day, let alone for the rest of my life. I considered myself lucky in at least two regards: I did not have the added responsibility of young children and of tending to their grief in addition to my own; and because we worked from home, I did not have to return to an office within weeks of his death. In fact, I would've had to quit my job, as there was no possible way I could have been a functional employee after so short a time. Starting in those early months in between much-needed weekend getaways with family and friends, I allowed myself long stretches of quiet time and went out of my way to make sure that my environment was as quiet as possible. My first order of business was to cancel our subscription to the local newspaper, and although Charlie and I used to watch the first twenty minutes of a morning news show to catch the top stories of the day, I stopped watching the news. I even stopped listening to National Public Radio, which we had both relished. My heart was already full to overflowing with misery and suffering; I didn't have the emotional capacity to listen to details about the misery and suffering going on in the world. I also stopped watching television every night, another one of our habits—even old movies.

Before I could fully reengage with the outside world, I knew that I needed to shine a light of self-compassion inward, onto me. Self-care and self-love became my priority. I sought refuge in words, those contained between book covers. Books and poetry about coping with, surviving, and accepting loss became my lifeline. Reading others' words on the subject of grief and learning how each had walked their own unique path through it acted as a cooling, soothing balm to my scorched heart.

I did most of my reading on a leather recliner in my living room that I came to refer to as my healing chair. I read more books and shed more tears here than in any other room in my house. From the chair, I had a direct view of a magnificent, towering cottonwood tree (which I came to name Gaia, and which I would journal about) growing in my neighbor's backyard. For the first two years especially, Gaia and I marched in lockstep through time: As she changed with the seasons, so was I transformed in my journey through grief.

I turned the living room into my sanctuary. I surrounded myself with objects and sounds that brought me peace and comfort: candles, incense, statues of Buddha—one of which I adorned with a gold chain that held our wedding bands—photos of Charlie, his ashes, meditation and nature CDs, a soft blanket, and my books. A small side table within arm's reach held a constant supply of tissues to absorb the river of tears and a phone, from which every day at precisely 3:30 p.m. MST, I would call my mom in Connecticut.

There are no words to express the gratitude and love I have for my mom. Throughout those desperate hours and days that turned into years, she gave so much of herself to me while, for much of the time, I was able to offer her very little beyond a lot of weeping. But she held the space for me every day and simply allowed me to be, however that presented itself in the moment. Just to be heard, even if I didn't have much to say, helped me to move my grief through and out of me. If I couldn't talk or didn't feel like talking on any particular day, she would talk for both of us. If all I could do was cry, she'd let me. It has never escaped me that Charlie's passing gave me the gift of knowing more about my mother and her life than I'd ever known. We laugh today about how both mother and daughter are now "wise old women." She is my greatest blessing.

When we are in deep grief, we must learn to hold ourselves with great love and compassion. We must shine the light inward, bask in it for a time, and let it warm us. When the seas are dark and stormy, and the waves are breaking over our bows, we need to find a safe harbor. We need a sanctuary, a place to take refuge from the storm. A comfortable place to sit, to drop into our bellies, to breathe and be quiet with ourselves; a place to cry; a place to *be;* a place where our broken spirit can begin to heal. If our sanctuary cannot be found in our home, then perhaps we can find it in our place of worship. If it cannot be found indoors, then the greatest sanctuary of all—Mother Nature—awaits right outside our door, open for business 24/7.

"The earth is my sister. I love her daily grace, her silent daring, and how loved I am. How we admire the strength in each other, all that we have lost, all that we have suffered, all that we know. We are stunned by this beauty, and I do not forget, what she is to me, what I am to her."
Susan Griffin

Other than my books, taking long daily walks became a vital part of my healing and self-care. Nature had donned her glorious springtime attire when tragedy entered my life, and I couldn't help but be drawn to her. She became my greatest healer and one of my greatest teachers, for it was on those walks with her that I first began to hear my still, inner voice. It whispered words of encouragement: *"Just keep breathing. Just keep walking. Just keep taking in, moment by precious moment, all of the glory and all of the beauty of this life. Just keep putting one foot in front of the other."*

Before too long, the voice within revealed the answer to my most pressing question, How will I ever survive this? I heard in reply, *"Just keep listening."* And when I did listen, I was blessed with the Divine gift of knowing that all the answers we seek are never "out there," but reside deep inside us and are revealed to us when we are quiet. As Isak Dinesen said, *"*Who tells a finer tale than any of us? Silence does."

Gradually, over time, tuning in to the frequency of this still, reassuring voice became easier. It helped me to come to a knowing, a surety, that if I *could* embrace each moment and reside within and breathe inside each—one by one by one as they unfolded—then I would survive the suicide death of my husband and my life, moving forward, would unfold precisely as it should. I came to know a power greater than myself but not separate from myself. And I began to trust that if I simply yielded to this greater power, to The One within, that I would always be faithfully guided toward the next step I needed to take on my journey. In those first years of my deep grief, my time spent in nature unlocked and opened an inner door that led me to a richer, deeper, more mindful, courageous, trusting, compassionate, loving, and grateful version of myself than I ever dreamed possible.

Nature herself is part of this greater power, for not only is she the greatest source of all that is beautiful, but she is also Our Mother, the giver of all of life. She nourishes us and reminds us that, like her, we have our own rhythms and our own seasons of life: from birth to growth to death to the promise of renewal. She is an eternal reminder that the light will faithfully return after even the darkest and bleakest night. She and we are of the same breath; we share the same life force energy; we are of the earth and one with the earth. Anytime we connect with her by walking through her and immersing ourselves in her, we connect with God in the midst of His creation—and in so doing, we connect with our still, inner voice: The One who knows.

"Earth Mother, you who are called by a thousand names. May all remember we are cells in your body and dance together."
Starhawk

Life seems to be one big call to action! We live in a frenzied world that demands our attention every single moment of our waking days. We make lists of everything we need to get done in the course of a day, but our checklists are never completed. In fact, they just keep getting longer. We're in constant motion, running as fast as we can toward some elusive goal line, but we find that no matter how fast we run, the world is still right there, nipping at our heels. We are rewarded for what we "do" for a living, so we "do" with no holds barred. We don't slow our pace, because we actually believe that we either can't or aren't allowed to. It's every man and woman for themselves.

So we keep running, never realizing that most of us are running on empty, never stopping long enough to replenish ourselves with the vital food that we need to feed and nourish our bodies and minds, let alone our hearts and souls. In our downtime, the world—which is more than ready, willing, and able to accommodate us—tempts us to partake in a million and one distractions meant to entertain us or to make us "feel better." And we gladly oblige. We anesthetize ourselves with food, drugs, sex, alcohol, television, sports, pornography, video games, shopping, cell phones, or social media. We've become a society of addicts. We consider all these distractions well-earned rewards for working so hard at the game of life, never realizing that they're all simply temporary fixes for whatever ails us.

And, we wonder, what exactly *is* it that ails us? *Something* niggles, calling out for our attention, but for the life of us, we can't seem to get a bead on exactly what that something is. We have this innate sense that someone, somewhere is trying to tell us something, something important. But we shake it off, convincing ourselves that it's nothing. Or maybe we're terrified that if we stop long enough to listen, this somewhat bothersome voice will tell us something we don't want to hear—so we keep stifling it with distractions, hoping it'll go away.

That niggling voice whispering to you is you—your Divine Guidance. Thirteenth century spiritual poet Rumi calls it the "second knowing" in his poem, "Two Kinds of Intelligence": "This second knowing is a fountainhead from within you, moving out." It's the voice that is waiting— *longing* to be heard. It's your life calling from the other side of the door. But to open the door and look at your life squarely in the face can be too scary and hard. It takes great courage. Most of us aren't that brave. So we keep ignoring it. We stand outside, with our hand on the knob, petrified to turn it.

But life can't be ignored forever. Pretty soon, like a pesky mosquito we keep shooing away, that niggling little voice is going to find its mark, and it's going to bite. The whisper will become a dull roar, and those little rap, tap, tappings from your inner door will become resounding booms. Life will demand our complete attention. No distraction will mask it. Nothing will tamp it down. We'll have nowhere to run, nowhere to hide. It will call upon us one day in such a way that we will no longer be able to ignore what it is trying to tell us.

Sadly, for most of us, me included, it's not until something devastating and profound happens to us that we finally "get it": we realize we need to leave the fast lane and seek a rest stop. Not only have we crashed headlong into an obstacle that wasn't on our map, we've totaled the car, leaving us stranded in the middle of a long, dark, lonely serpentine highway—the highway of grief that we're now forced to navigate alone. It is then that we will have to find and use our inner compass if we are ever to make our way back home.

We can derive a measure of comfort, particularly in our times of despair, if we remain mindful of the fact that everything in life, including our pain and suffering, is impermanent. And if we can take our pain and suffering inward and sit with it for a while in the quiet—knowing that it shall pass—our heart light will ignite and begin to illuminate our way.

Grieving, by its very nature, pulls us inward. It is there we retreat in our times of quiet and solitude. And it is there, inside us, where the buried gifts of our sorrow and loss—a treasure trove of gifts, in fact—lay hidden, waiting to be discovered. These gifts are priceless but remain elusive unless and until we surrender to our pain and our sorrow, until we allow our grief to move through us and carry us to where our treasure resides: inside our broken heart. It is there, buried deep within, where these lustrous pearls of wisdom await, there for the taking. Each of us who is grieving possesses the treasure map to these gems, and the map reveals one clue that, if followed, all but guarantees that to the victor will go the spoils.

The one clue is this: Enter the silence. Once there, everything will be made clear. In time, those buried pearls will be uncovered and will begin to yield to us and impart their wisdom. The more we listen, the more treasure we will be blessed with. This holds true whether we have experienced a loss or not.

For me, as soon as I discovered the "clue" of silence during one of my daily walks, I began turning inward and listening for and to my still, inner voice. Those precious pearls began rising to the surface. Here are two of the most priceless ones that revealed themselves: One imparted to me not just the feeling but the absolute belief that I could and would have a meaningful life after Charlie's death; the other imparted to me the absolute knowing that I was meant to write this book. As I grieved, it was Silence and Nature that bestowed upon me their greatest treasure and their greatest blessing: Wisdom. I pray that you might allow both to do the same for you as you heal.

"We need to find God, and he cannot be found in the noise and restlessness. God is the friend of silence. See how nature—trees, flowers, grass—grow in silence; see the stars, the moon and the sun—how they move in silence. … We need silence to be able to touch souls."
Mother Teresa

In her beautiful book *I Will Not Die an Unlived Life*, author Dawna Markova writes:

"Retreating into oneself to find purpose is like straddling a boat leaving a dock, pulled in opposite directions by the intense desire of the mind for human involvement and the equally intense need of the soul for its own company. In the sheer immensity of solitude, when one can no longer draw energy from external sources, we come to see how much of what we habitually call meaningful purpose is merely the evasion of sitting still and meeting what is most difficult for us to receive with compassion—our own pain."

In *A Grief Observed*, C. S. Lewis's moving and tender account of his journey through grief upon the death of his beloved wife "H," he describes an event that "H" experienced before they were married. "H was haunted all one morning as she went about her work with the obscure sense of God (so to speak) 'at her elbow,' demanding her attention. And, of course, not being a perfected saint, she had the feeling that it would be a question, as it usually is, of some unrepented sin or tedious duty. At last she gave in—I know how one puts it off—and faced Him. But the message was, 'I want to give you something' and instantly she entered into joy."

God sought to give H what He wishes to give all of us: his gifts of grace, joy, hope, compassion, faith, gratitude, charity, guidance, reassurance, strength, courage, resilience, fortitude, comfort, peace, forgiveness, wellness, healing, and His boundless, unconditional love. He resides within the niggling, whispering voice we hear deep down, and He is there always—just on the other side of the door, praying that we turn the knob and cross the threshold into the stillness, where he and his infinite treasure trove of gifts await.

"The soul lives there in the silent breath."
Rumi

Nature and Silence are blessings to me. Today I continue to spend as much time as possible in both places. I never did restart my subscription to the newspaper. As far as television goes, I continue to watch very little news—just enough to know what's going on in the world—and I have gradually begun recording and watching a few, select favorite programs and movies, many of them comedies, as I am a firm believer that laughter is the best medicine. I continue to value and cherish the time I spend being *still* and listening for and to that little voice within, the voice of wisdom and of truth, the voice of The One.

"Our grief has yielded a wisdom that can see into the way the world shapes us through our time of loss." *Francis Weller*, The Wild Edge of Sorrow: Rituals of Renewal and the Sacred Work of Grief

* * *

As you grieve, may you seek solace not only in the company of others, but also in your own company and in the company of Nature, where you can enter the quiet and still your restless mind and calm your restless heart. And may you not fear the Silence, but embrace it, knowing that it has so much to teach you if you will but listen. Amen.

"Forgive others, not because they deserve forgiveness, but because you deserve peace."
Unknown

II

The Blessing of Forgiveness

"The truth is, unless you let go, unless you forgive yourself, unless you forgive the situation, unless you realize that the situation is over, you cannot move forward."
Steve Maraboli, *Unapologetically You: Reflections on Life and the Human Experience*

A FEW WEEKS AFTER CHARLIE DIED, I didn't think that I could descend any further into the dark abyss of grief or that my heart could break any more than it already had. But I was mistaken. One day, as I began going through his "things," I happened upon his journals in his nightstand. Several years earlier, Charlie had begun keeping a daily gratitude journal. No matter how challenging any given day might have been for him, he would write down everything he was grateful for. I was fully aware of and pleased by his dedication to his practice, and I looked upon his journals as one would a diary: as sacrosanct.

And so when I came across them, I took them out of the drawer and held them as though they were antique books that demanded to be treated with the utmost delicacy, as if they'd crumble to dust in my hands if I opened them. I looked upon his journals as inviolable: if I read even one entry, I would somehow be betraying Charlie and his trust. But I did. Even today, I'm not sure I did the right thing, because reading them only led to more heartbreak.

When someone takes their own life, there is a lot of collateral damage. Friends and especially family members are encumbered not only by their overwhelming grief, but also by their overwhelming anger and guilt. I was heavily burdened by all three, but his journals would compound my guilt a hundredfold. Peppered throughout them were entries about his struggle to "stay." One, dated in 2013, two years before he died, said, "I am grateful that I am no longer thinking about departure."

Soon after finding his journals, I went into Charlie's computer to look for a business-related folder. During my search, I was shocked to discover letters he had written to me and placed in a folder for me to find, entitled "Important Stuff." (I mention this file in a bit more detail in the next chapter, "The Blessing of Affirmations.") But what was more shocking was to discover that he'd begun composing them in 2013, and the last modification to the *personal* letter he'd left for me to find was made two days before he died.

My sister Kathy would later inform me that the day he died, the detective she talked to on the phone said that the EMTs had found a note on Charlie. In the chaos, Kathy couldn't recall if he'd said anything more about it. For whatever reason, that note was never given to me by the authorities, and no one remembered to inquire about it again.

It was all but forgotten until I discovered it that day. It was dated, not surprisingly, March 30, 2013, and last modified on October 28, 2014. It explained why he'd chosen to take his life at the VA hospital. Because a firearm had been discharged, his death was first treated as a crime, because for all the authorities knew, Charlie could have been murdered. (In addition, because too much time had elapsed before it was determined that a suicide had been committed, it was impossible to harvest any of his organs. But I did receive a call from University Hospital in Denver a few weeks later, telling me that they were able to harvest some of his skin tissue. That news made my heart sing.) Charlie seemed to be aware of the consequences of his actions in his letter:

I apologize for all the inconvenience the necessity of using such a messy method of suicide may cause. I have chosen to do this near the emergency room entrance to the VA hospital in the hopes that you will be able to harvest more of my organs and tissue having my body immediately upon my death. I hope this makes up for the mess I will have created in doing so. NOTE: Per my living will, <u>I do not want to be put on any life support</u> whatsoever. Take what you can, but again, no life support!! Please call my wife Karen at ....

I was devastated by these revelations: he'd been planning his suicide for years! To know this now when it was too late ... I so, *so* wished I'd known it then! I deeply believed that I *should* have known something was terribly off with him, and this conviction just about crippled me. Now, in addition to the insurmountable weight of my immense grief, I shouldered the weight of self-recrimination that bordered on self-loathing. The internalized anger that I should have projected onto Charlie for leaving me, for abandoning me, for betraying me, for never sharing with me what he had long planned to do so that I could have helped him—I now projected onto myself and others. *How could I not have known something was wrong? What did I miss? Where was I all this time? How could I not have seen this coming?* After all, I was the one who spent 23 years with this man, glued at the hip, 24/7. I was convinced that I was living in a fairy tale, when all the while my "Prince Charming" was living in a nightmare. How could the love of my life keep the love of his life completely in the dark? How could he have held it all together on the outside for so long, while dying a slow and painful death on the inside—and being resolute about one day taking his own life? I knew our love was deep and strong, and I'd always believed it would be enough to sustain us for the rest of our lives, come what may. But in the end, it hadn't been enough to keep him here. This realization added one more layer to the shroud of grief that crushed me.

From all outward appearances, Charlie had exuded happiness and an air of confidence. Everyone who met him took an instant liking to him. Energetically, he was a bright light illuminating the space he occupied, and people were naturally drawn to him. But inside, his spirit was in great turmoil. A war had begun; exactly when and why it began, no one but Charlie would ever know. From his journals, the battle for his soul had raged for at least three years, during which time he made a lionhearted attempt to vanquish this inner demon; but in the end, his foe won.

Author Steffany Barton, who possesses the gift of listening to the voices of departed loved ones, writes in her book, *Facing Darkness, Finding Light: Life After Suicide,* "Those who are left behind after a death by suicide are challenged to find a profound level of courage and faith as they learn to accept that they are guiltless in the suicide and not to blame for the death of another." And then, "When is suicide not preventable? If suicide has occurred." She says further, "I want to bring to light a singular truth: those who commit suicide could not have been stopped, or the suicide would not have occurred. ... In accepting this, guilt shall be washed away, those survivors, imprisoned by shame, shall once and for all be set free."

Being a suicide survivor, I cannot tell you how much comfort and relief reading these words—and her entire book—gave me. There is no preventing suicide. Period. Believing this to be true did wash away much of the stain of guilt and shame that I carried. And although I'd had no problem whatsoever taking my anger out on God early on in my grieving, her book didn't help me assuage the anger that I felt toward Charlie—anger that stayed buried deep in my subconscious for months before rearing its ugly head. Coming to grips with and releasing this most deep-seated and challenging emotion would require different tools from my grief toolbox: individual therapy and time. Lots of time. Even today, I know I still carry residual suppressed anger toward Charlie. Prior to his departure, I rarely had angry outbursts. But since his death, I find that at times, I misdirect my anger, guilt, shame, and feelings of abandonment and betrayal toward those I love the most. And when I do this, it leaves me feeling horrible. After four years, most of my wounds have not only scabbed over, but left scars. I pray that time will eventually heal my misdirected emotions.

"I sat with my anger long enough until she told me her real name was grief."
Unknown

Granted, my personal challenge to overcome guilt and anger, and to forgive myself and Charlie for his death, is from the perspective of a suicide survivor. We lose our loved ones in myriad ways: accidents, illness, old age, by their own hand, or by the hands of another. When a loved one is taken by the hands of another, the survivors are left with the herculean task of forgiving the unforgivable, adding an extra, unfathomable layer of pain and suffering to their grieving process.

That said, no matter *how* the person passed, our first task is to forgive them for dying and for leaving us behind. If, while they lived, they trespassed against us, we need to find a way to now forgive them their trespasses. If we believe we had trespassed against them while they lived, we need to find a way to forgive ourselves our trespasses. If we find ourselves railing at our God for having taken our loved one and we lose our faith, then we must find a way, in the face of our pain, suffering, guilt and remorse, to make room in our hearts for the blessings of mercy and compassion. For without mercy and compassion, our faith in ourselves, our lost loved one, or in our God can never be fully restored.

"Holding on to anger is like grasping a hot coal with the intent of throwing it at someone else; you are the one who gets burned."
Buddha

We must find a way, someday, somehow, to replace our anger and self-flagellation with reconciliation. We need to reconcile with our past, for the past cannot be changed. The past no longer matters, because the past no longer exists. The only thing that exists is this moment, right here, right now. It is in this moment when each of us is presented the opportunity to come to that place of forgiveness. To continually punish ourselves, or to stay in a limbo of "shoulda-coulda-wouldas" or what-ifs, is self-torture and self-sabotage and only succeeds in preventing us from advancing on our journey. If, in order to move through these emotions and prevent them from paralyzing us, we need to seek professional advice or religious or spiritual counsel, then that is what we must do. We must arrive at a place of understanding that forgiveness is a gift to ourselves and is the very cord that binds the wound of our broken heart and allows us to live and love again.

When we experience a loss, almost every human emotion or feeling imaginable is unleashed. Just a few of the most challenging are: sadness, shame, regret, fear, denial, guilt, anger, hopelessness, loneliness, betrayal, abandonment, disbelief, shock, longing, and despair. Each can be compared to one head of the mythological Greek monster Lernaean Hydra. The Hydra had many heads, and every time someone would cut one of them off, two more heads would grow out of the stump. Those of us who are grieving find ourselves lopping off head after head as we move through our emotions, hoping to at least quell, if not outright vanquish, them. If, as we move forward on our individual paths, we are to reach the final signposts of forgiveness and acceptance, then we must be brave and, without flinching, lop off as many heads as are required to get there.

"Grief can be the garden of compassion. If you keep your heart open through everything, your pain can become your greatest ally in your life's search for love and wisdom."
Rumi

* * *

Early on, the loss of your loved one can fill you with guilt, remorse, and anger. These emotions encapsulate your heart like a prison wall through which no light can penetrate. Thus imprisoned, the heart becomes hardened, closed, and embittered. As you move forward on your path, may you allow your grief to dismantle your prison wall, one brick at a time, and set your heart free. And in place of that prison, may you build a beautiful, holy temple to enshrine your tender, open, loving, compassionate, forgiving heart. And know this, it is forgiveness that leads us back to love and is our liberation and salvation. Amen.

"This too shall pass."
Attar of Nishapur, Sufi poet, circa 1200 CE

12

The Blessing of

Affirmations

"Let go and let God."
Philippians 4:6–7

THE LATE LOUISE HAY, American motivational author and founder of Hay House, said this about the power of positive affirmations: "An affirmation opens the door. It's a beginning point on the path to change. In essence, you're saying to your subconscious mind, 'I am taking responsibility, I am aware that there is something I can do to change.'"

Charlie was a Marine who served in Vietnam, and soldiers are all about being prepared. In combat, their very lives depend on it. Charlie was extremely handy and always had a project going—making or fixing something, either for us or for family and friends. He reveled in staying busy. For him, it was all about having the right gear or the right tool for any job or any occasion. Whenever a family or friend lacked something essential to complete a project, he would get a call. They were certain he would have just what they needed—and most often he did, right down to the exact nut or bolt. Like a magician pulling a rabbit out of a hat, he'd pull the needed item out of his ditty bag, which he carried with him everywhere, or his well-stocked garage (can you say "hoarder"?). "Mr. Boy Scout" was often lovingly teased about the level of his preparedness, but he took great pride in it.

Even in death, he left prepared. Two days after he died, I found a letter from him to me sticking out of the bottom drawer of our filing cabinet. So beautifully typical of Charlie, his letter contained directions to the whereabouts of an entire folder, within which were a personal letter to his son—my stepson—another lengthy letter entitled "Technical Stuff," and one entitled "Financial Stuff." The last two were chock-full of invaluable information that he knew I would need and upon which I relied for many months afterward. I was never more grateful to him for his preparedness!

On April 6, 2015, the day he left me and the world for good, Charlie told me he had scheduled a last-minute business appointment, which wasn't true but he did it in order to leave without rousing my suspicions. He even added the bogus appointment to his Outlook schedule for me to find. The irony would not be lost on me when I later got a copy of his death certificate: by the time I even *thought* to look at his computer, he had already died.

When the time came for Charlie to leave the house that day, I was sitting on the grass in our backyard enjoying the fine spring day. He came to the screen door and simply said goodbye. As it was already almost half past one, I asked him if he was sure he was going to be able to make it back by 3 for dinner. He assured me that he would. I heard our garage door open and close. I decided to go inside, where I shuffled around the kitchen for ten or so minutes, gathering the ingredients I needed to prepare a new pasta recipe I planned to serve. But the beautiful day was beckoning. I let our two cats, Fumo and Smudge, out, and the three of us were sitting on the grass when I heard the garage door open again.

Charlie called out to me that he'd forgotten something upstairs on his desk and disappeared. He reappeared a couple of minutes later and hollered out, "See you soon!" and left. Those were his last spoken words to me.

Maybe it's just wishful thinking, but I'd like to believe that he stood at the screen door watching me and our cats, drinking us in one last time for just a few more moments before saying his final, parting words.

Charlie died on a Monday. The next day, I composed a fairly lengthy letter to email to our out-of-state family and friends that attempted to explain Charlie's decision to take his own life, even though I had not yet found his letter to me. Then, two weeks later, a strange thing happened. I opened Microsoft Word for the first time since writing that letter and clicked on "Recently Viewed Documents." My letter was at the very top but the next file was one called "I Love You." It was a Valentine's card that Charlie had made for me on his computer years before, a document that had been buried so deep in our network files that I didn't even remember it being there. On a plain white background, in rainbow colors, he'd written in a rather large font, "I LOVE YOU BEST BUDDY!!—and in a smaller font was "More than words could ever express!! Forever Your Me." At the time, he'd left a printed copy of it on my keyboard for me to find.

How had this document found its way to the top of the files? I didn't know, but my broken heart soared. My beloved had found a way to communicate with me from the other side. It was another miracle! Tears of joy and gratitude burst from my eyes. I fell to my knees and thanked him over and over again.

As ecstatic as I was to read those three precious words from Charlie one last time, darker thoughts soon overshadowed the joy. I sat in my office that morning and began to wonder about his final day. What state of mind was he in as he began his journey to the VA hospital, his final destination? What had it been like for him? I wondered what his eyes had taken in. Had he opened a window to breathe in the warm spring air? Had he felt the benevolent sun shining on him through the windows of his truck—which he had named Lucky—warming him for a final time? Had he seen and appreciated the beauty of the trees and bushes that were beginning to blossom? He had to have been running on pure adrenaline, all of his senses heightened to the max, bombarded with *life* one last time. Or was his life passing before his eyes even as he drove? Was he completely numb and oblivious to his surroundings, like he was having an out-of-body experience? Was he like someone who drives drunk, gets home, and doesn't remember how they got there? Or, through the grace of God, was he already in a state of limbo, half in this world and half in the other, in a protective state of shock? I will live the rest of my life wondering.

On the day I discovered that file, I firmly believed that I was witness to some sort of miracle; like there truly was some ghost in my machine, and the ghost was Charlie. But within a few months, I came to know two things. One is that I wouldn't have noticed that file the day I composed my letter to family and friends because I was immersed in the embryonic stages of acute grief and shock; it was all I could do to focus on the task at hand. And two, I was blessed with an "aha!" moment while talking about it for the umpteenth time with a family member: the card was the reason Charlie had come back to the house that day.

Once I knew this in my heart, I was both moved and stunned by the amount of courage and mental preparedness it must have taken for him to steel himself for what he was about to do: to begin that long, one-way drive to eternity and then, suddenly, ten minutes into it, have the presence of mind to remember that he'd forgotten *one* final and very important detail—maybe in his mind, the most important detail of all. He'd forgotten to pull that file up on my computer so that I would find it, so that I would be able to hear the words he knew I'd be longing and needing to hear one more time: I love you. Mr. Boy Scout wasn't about to let that happen. So he'd turned his truck around and drove those ten minutes and however many miles back to the house to dot that final "i" and cross that final "t."

No, I cannot begin to comprehend, nor will I ever know the depth of the psychic pain and anguish that he had to be experiencing that day as he got behind the wheel of his beloved truck and began driving away from me. What is even more incomprehensible is how in the midst of his own terror and anguish he could even *remember* this one last detail. He'd added another twenty agonizing minutes to his drive that day, and he'd done that for me. This beautiful, selfless gesture was his last, but greatest testament of his love.

On that beautiful Sunday morning when I found his Valentine, I *felt* him, his very presence, in the room with me. I remember turning my chair around to face his, as I'd done for countless years. Through the gauze of tears that fogged my vision, I imagined Charlie sitting right there, no more

149

than four feet away, beaming at me with his warm, beautiful smile—a smile so big and bright that it made his blue eyes, also wet with tears, crinkle. He was determined to be there with me to share those brief moments of profound joy that he knew this last gesture would bestow upon me in the midst of the pain and suffering that he'd also left me with. For the first time since he died, a sense of deep peace and calm enveloped my heart.

My husband had saved his last and best magic trick for last. In his eleventh hour, in those agonizing extra twenty minutes, he'd found a way to pull the rabbit out of his hat to tell me one last time that he loved me. Sometimes, even the most tragic acts can generate hidden gifts.

I printed out his card that day and placed it on my refrigerator. That was the beginning. For the next two-plus years, my refrigerator became a giant magnet for affirmations: poems, sentences, song lyrics, single words, phrases, or paragraphs from the many books I was reading at the time. I would hang and rotate forty-five different affirmations; I know the exact number, because I saved them all in a folder. In fact, as I write this, one affirmation remains after four years: "Allow what is to be." The words in all of those affirmations were powerful tools that aided me tremendously in my healing.

I once read a quip, "A smile is one step closer to laughing." While at the time, laughter seemed a distant memory, I did manage to derive a few smiles from a bright yellow smiley-faced clock that I'd bought early on to hang above my desk and that still manages to turn my frown upside down. And like the clock, reading the affirmations over and over again like a mantra for days, weeks, months, and years helped rewire the circuitry in my brain. It was like my brain was being bombarded with thousands of bright yellow smiley-faced clocks, and they were staving off dark black frowny-faced clocks that were trying to infiltrate. And for family and friends who visited on a regular basis, my rotating affirmations over those years acted as a touchstone by which they were able to track the progress of my grief and my healing, which helped make *them* feel better too!

Many of my affirmations were song lyrics and poetry by others, but here are a few of my own:

"I'm doing the best that I can."
"The best way out of it is through it."
"Relax your mind. Sit. Listen inside. Let go. Have no worries. Know this. You are loved."
"It is what it is."
"Stay in the 'is-ness' of the moment."
"If the dream I had can no longer be, it's time to dream a different dream."
"Right now, I don't need to know anything!"
"Trust. Allow. Imagine. Receive. Believe. Know. Love."
"I am safe. I am protected. I am loved. I am not alone."
"I trust in God's Divine plan for me."
"Let go!"
"Let it be!"
"You're doing great, Karen!"
"Think of what you had instead of what you lost."
"I will continue to keep my arms open and I will continue to surrender."

151

"Trust. Allow. Accept. Believe. And know that I am still doing the best that I can."
"Embrace. Surrender. My journey is my own."
"Healing hurts. Hurting heals."
"You gotta feel it to heal it!"
"Suffering is resisting the moment."
"The Light always wins."
"He stayed as long as he could."
"I'm still doing the best that I can."
"In this moment, I am exactly where I'm supposed to be."

Louie Schwartzberg, the world's preeminent nature cinematographer, writes about the magic of words in his book *Mindful Intentions*: "Words are powerful. So much of who we are, what we do, and how we live is framed and forged by language. Even when the goal is to clear and calm the mind, words can be put to use very effectively. This is how we come to our Mindful Intentions." A Mindful intention, he writes, "is a word, phrase, or sentence that's used as a cue to help the mind focus, to shine that 'mental flashlight' on a singular, purposeful thought."

Words are arguably the most powerful force available to humans. The curriculum of *A Course in Miracles* poses that *all* thoughts create form on some level and that they can lead us to either heaven or hell. The words we choose to think, speak, or write can act as agents of positive change or of destructive thought patterns. When we are in the throes of grief, it is especially important that we choose our words carefully, for our thoughts can be a conduit of either further healing or of deeper pain and suffering.

* * *

Whether you write them, read them, think them, or speak them, may the affirmations you surround yourself with as you grieve your loss consist of words that inspire, encourage, empower, and comfort you. And may you write, read, think, or speak them repeatedly, and in so doing, know that these words are acting as powerful catalysts for healing and for radical change. Remember: The same crack in a door that lets the rain in lets the sunshine in too. And while it's true that rain is necessary for growth, so too is sunshine. Sorrow can make you feel as though your cracked heart is wrapped within dark, dense rain clouds that pummel it with torrents that seem never to let up. Think of your positive affirmations as fierce warriors, each armed with a sunbeam whose sole mission is to clear away the clouds and wrap your heart in the warmth of the sun, allowing you to grow as you grieve. Amen.

The Divine Simplicity of Breath

What is this secret wonder
stirring in stone-hearted grief,
dissolving prison walls,
pouring out in a cloud of glimmering wings?
What alchemy turns sullen tears
to bells ringing in a vast sky,
refusal and choked breath
to a flowing symphony of light?
Each in-drawn breath
lights a thousand candles,
opens the doors of vaulted mansions,
walks toward quiet water at twilight.
The in-drawn, forgiving breath
enters the world awaiting creation,
fills the chalice
with the spaciousness of stars,
breathes out holiness.

Sherri Rose-Walker, 2008

Karen Trench

13

The Blessing of Acceptance

"Life moves on, whether we act as cowards or heroes. Life has no other discipline to impose, if we could but realize it, than to accept life unquestioningly. Everything we shut our eyes to, everything we run away from, everything we deny, denigrate or despise, serves to defeat us in the end. What seems nasty, painful, evil, can become a source of beauty, joy and strength, if faced with an open mind. Every moment is a golden one for him who has the vision to recognize it as such."
Henry Miller

YEARS AGO, MY SISTER PRISCILLA tragically lost her husband in a motorcycle accident. Imprinted on my brain is the vision of her sobbing uncontrollably and telling me how her life felt like a blank TV screen that only yesterday was airing a romantic movie with a happy ending. In an instant, fate had turned the switch, the screen had gone black, and she was certain that she'd never again be able to envision another picture appearing on it. When Charlie died, I felt the exact same way.

When we're in the throes of grief, it's not only incomprehensible, but impossible to imagine a life without our loved one to share it—let alone try to reimagine a future for ourselves. And yet life does indeed move on, whether we want it to or not. As Aristotle once said, "Nature abhors a vacuum." As soon as one thing is emptied out, a space is created for something else to fill it.

The ritual of grieving in and of itself can make us feel disempowered, victimized, and at the mercy of our pain and suffering. But at some point on our journey, we begin to realize that as much as we might long for the life that once was, our new reality dictates we must begin to imagine the unimaginable: building a new life without the presence of our lost loved one. This seemingly impossible feat is one of the hidden blessings of grief and loss, for it is the one aspect of our grieving over which we have some measure of control. We get to choose how to fill and occupy the space that our loss has created, and the ability to choose is empowering. The void will be filled regardless, so it's best if we consciously choose how *best* to fill it. The possibilities are endless!

"When we are wounded we carry it until it grounds us. We writhe and call and fight the wind—until we move with it."
Natalie Costanza-Chavez

But how do we begin to pick up the pieces of our shattered lives and move forward? One morning, we will awake, and our shroud of grief will feel lighter, as it did for author C. S. Lewis. In *A Grief Observed,* he writes: "Something quite unexpected happened. It came this morning early. For various reasons, not in themselves mysterious, my heart was lighter than it had been for many weeks. ... And suddenly at that very moment when, so far, I mourned H. [his wife] least, I remembered her best. ... It was as if the lifting of sorrow removed a barrier."

It was on that particular day, in the light of a new dawn, that Lewis arrived at the final signpost on his grief journey: Acceptance, identified by psychiatrist Elisabeth Kübler-Ross in her book *On Death and Dying*. He had made peace with the loss of his beloved wife.

Each of us arrives at the place of Acceptance in our own way and in our own time. We will know that we've arrived if we can honestly answer *"yes,"* with our heart and not our head, to the question that this place will ask of us: Is the risk of remaining rooted in this spot, looking back longingly on a life that was but can no longer be, more painful than looking ahead to a life of new possibilities?

If our answer is "yes," then we need to pat ourselves on the back, for we have, as Lewis did that morning, wholly assimilated and integrated the loss of our loved one into our very being. When we reach this step, it is as though we see our life and our lost loved one more clearly and with renewed vision. Thus both our life and our loved one become that much more beloved and precious to us. We may even begin to imagine the possibility of welcoming in another emotion that has been concealed in the dark folds of our pain, one we thought we'd never feel again: joy!

"Joy lives concealed in grief."
Rumi

Our grief for our lost loved one never goes away entirely; it's simply transmuted. For the rest of our lives, it will, from time to time, resurface and knock us back down a few steps. But the integration of our loss becomes synonymous with having reached the pinnacle of our grief journey. After our arduous climb, sooner or later we summit! And once there, there's no going back or staying back for too long. For we know that we have grieved the loss of our loved one passionately and well. That we have become reconciled to our grief. That our grief has now melted into who we are: a happy, loving person who has experienced loss. And that although our grief has torn us apart, it has alchemized us, transformed us, and given us the opportunity to reinvent ourselves and our lives.

Grief tears us apart so that we can re-create ourselves. But the person we create is entirely up to us. We, all of us, are the choices we make. We can choose to let our grief defeat us or let it elevate us. We can choose to become angry and embittered by our loss, or we can choose to surrender to it—heart, mind, body, and soul—and let it take us where we need to go. We can choose to resist it, or we can choose to allow it to peel back all the layers of our pain and suffering so that something beautiful and unique can be revealed. Loss can bring us closer to death or closer to life. It can bring us closer to the dark or closer to the light. It can vanquish us or resurrect us. It is our choice, every step of the way.

"Somewhere along the way, you do your best. And then you surrender. Let go...It is not powerlessness. It is freedom. Like you're in a dark room and it's light outside. Surrender means cleaning the window so that light can enter. You're letting the light enter, not

making it enter. It is not giving up, it is accepting. And the light will enter. Always does."
Kamal Ravikant, Live Your Truth

As a suicide survivor, I had a unique challenge. I needed to accept that I was alone and would be living the rest of my life without Charlie, but I also had to try to find some way to accept the choice he'd made. The surrendering of his possessions early on was the catalyst that forced me to acknowledge the hard, cold fact that my husband was dead and would never again return. But I had a long way to go before I could accept the way he died.

The road that would eventually lead me to that place of Acceptance began on day one when the detective informed me that Charlie was gone. In that moment, God delivered me immediately into a state of shock. Shock is an interesting phenomenon, something I had never experienced at such a profound level, and I felt cloaked in a protective bubble. I sat on my couch for what seemed like hours, in complete quiet and stillness, while my sister Kathy continued the gruesome task of calling friends and family. I remained like that even as the house began to fill with some of those same people. I do remember feeling extremely peaceful, calm, and safe in that place. I also vaguely recall being on the receiving end of a lot of compassion and sympathy—arms wrapped around me, hugging me, holding me, soothing me, and consoling me; soft words of regret and encouragement being murmured in my ear. While I don't recall exactly what those words were, I do remember feeling very loved.

The cocoon of shock and the enormous outpouring of support and sympathy that first night were, in hindsight, two of the saving graces that set me firmly on the long road I would need to walk in order to reconcile the suicide death. Another saving grace was when, on the second night, our dear friend Logan brought clairvoyant Tricia McCannon to my home. I write more about this experience in the chapter "The Journey Begins," but she was the first of many gifted healers whom God and Universe guided me to—every one of whom would become the wind at my back that pushed me further toward reconciliation and finally to Acceptance. What propelled me even faster toward this signpost were the dozens of books I read about grief and loss (also detailed in that chapter) and how other people just like me had navigated through it. At the time, in those early stages of acute grief, I just needed to *know* that like them, I could and would survive my loss. Their words reassured me on both counts.

Nevertheless, my path was not without obstacles. In the first five months my protective bubble of shock had carried me along like a seagull being carried by the tide. At the six-month mark, complications began to crop up when another protective bubble, the one of grief, began to dissolve. At eight months, the bubble had completely dissolved, putting me face-to-face with reality and life. It was then that the magnitude of my loss hit me. Up until that point, I had been willing and able to make allowances around Charlie's choice; now, that suddenly morphed into a new feeling: anger. In the early months of my grief journey, I would raise my fists beseechingly to God and asking, "Why? Why? Why?" Now I found myself on my knees asking Charlie the same thing. "I don't understand!" "Why?" "How could you do this to me?" "How could you be so selfish?" "How could you just leave me like this?" "Why couldn't you have talked to me first?" "Wasn't our love enough to keep you here?"

It would take me many months and ultimately therapy before I could fully acknowledge my strong feelings of anger, along with deep feelings of abandonment, shame, betrayal, and worthlessness. And because I had been stifling these painful feelings, I misdirected my anger at others, which I regret doing. With the help of a therapist, I came to realize that although I *never* would have agreed with Charlie's decision to end his life, the choice was not mine to make. And even though I never would have condoned it, it didn't mean that I couldn't accept it.

In the final analysis, we cannot ever really know why our loved one was taken from us at a particular time in a particular way. And yet, it is my firm belief that unless and until we come to a place of Acceptance, we will be left with an open wound that will fester for the rest of our lives and might even kill us. At best, our inability to reconcile our loss will continually be acted out like a Shakespearean tragedy in the Theater of Relationships.

It's safe to say that in many ways—perhaps in most ways—I am not the same woman who inhabited my body on April 6, 2015. On that day, in that moment when I got the horrible news, my vessel emptied out—the vessel that contained my very essence—and every atom that had made me who I was alchemized and then refilled my vessel with something entirely new and different.

After nearly four years, the woman I've become enjoys a deeper faith and connection to God and a spiritual practice that brings her great peace and joy and allows her to feel a connectedness to all of life. She has become a writer, a yoga practitioner, and a meditator, and she has aspirations to travel the world. And although no longer together, she met a lovely man who turned on the light in her heart and taught her how to be vulnerable to loving and being loved again, for which she will remain eternally grateful.

There is something to be said for carrying the mantle of survivor, whatever it is that we've survived—accident, illness, or loss. I suppose it's true that we never know how we will react to a tragedy until tragedy strikes. The only thing we can do when it does is our very best. Nothing more, nothing less. I could never have imagined just how much fortitude, courage, and emotional and spiritual strength I could muster in the face of my tragedy. Today, I feel stronger and more capable in every way. I believe with all my heart that what got me through was the moment, early on, when I surrendered myself over to what had happened to me— wholly and completely, with faith and trust that I was being guided, watched over, and protected at all times.

That is not to say that once I surrendered, I was able to remain in that sweet place. Quite the contrary. I found that surrendering wasn't a one-time choice; I needed to choose to surrender over and over and over again. I reverted back to fear and resistance numerous times on my journey. But when I found myself in that not-so-sweet place, I would bring my awareness to it and as quickly as I could, acknowledge my fear and suffering and then release it, knowing that's where peace lies. In time, I was able to stay *there* far more often, trusting that God and Universe had my back.

In retrospect, it was the path of Surrender that became my most direct one to the final path of Acceptance, where now, four years later, I can honestly say that I have fully accepted the loss of Charlie. And although I will never agree with his choice, I accept it. When I allowed what *was* to simply *be*, I found peace.

* * *

That we grieve is a given. How we grieve is a choice. May you choose to honor and embrace your grief and allow it to guide you where it will and to teach you what it will. From the moment your journey begins—in a place called Denial—to your arrival at your last stop called Acceptance, however long that might take, for every moment between and beyond, may you love yourself the whole way through as though your very life depends on it. Because it does! Amen.

Return From Exile

In these rooms time slows,
sound is muted,
light pauses for reverie;
<u>sub rosa</u> secrets slowly emerge,
ripening the moment to revelation.
Notes of harmonious clarity
distilled from dear chaos
weave interlace of dark and light,
grief-laced joy.
No trumpet fanfare
announces return from exile,
surrender to love.
Only new wind
blowing from east of the sun
and west of the moon
reanimates the kindly air
with green possibility.

Sherri Rose-Walker, 2018

14

The Blessing of Moving

Forward

Karen Trench

170

"As you start to walk on the way, the way appears."
Rumi

JUST BEFORE THE ONE-YEAR ANNIVERSARY of Charlie's
death, I wrote in my journal:

Some days I just want to run as fast as I can ... not
forward, but back to you. This moving forward without you,
into the unknown, all alone, is terrifying. I am so full of fear
that I'm not handling your leaving very well, that I'm not
navigating my own life very well at all. I'm full of doubt and
insecurity when all I want and what you deserve me to be is
a woman who can dust herself off, pick up the pieces of her
shattered heart, and be okay; to be more confident that
more good things await me. Please help me, sweetie. Please
watch over me and keep me strong. Help me to release any
fear and doubt. Help me to truly reach a place of surrender,
acceptance, and belief. Help me to be able to open my heart
to receive all of the love that flows inside and outside of me.
I love you and at times miss you terribly. I wish I could run
as fast as I can into your open arms, to the life that we shared.

After a great loss, it is our natural tendency to take
refuge in the past. Often, we give up our heart to it and cling
to it for dear life. We spend countless hours, days, months,
or even years with one wish: that we could turn back the
hands of time to when our loved one was still with us. Our
minds know that what we seek is impossible, but that

doesn't stop our hearts from longing. The shock of our loss can be so absolute and profound that we may find ourselves paralyzed—unsure of how we're going to navigate the next minute, let alone the next hour or next day. Our fear about life and its unpredictability can take root, and we begin to believe that we will never recover—that our life will never be anything more than what it has become since our loss: a life of immeasurable sorrow. We begin dwelling in a world of what-ifs.

In her book, *Sacred Lines: A Personal Journey from Darkness to Light*, Elizabeth Adams writes, "Once you fall into darkness, the fear, it becomes a difficult place to leave. The weariness, the density, become familiar. And yet the light is always on. Just reach for it."

When we are grieving, looking back to the life that *was* is far more comforting than looking ahead. The past is where we feel safe. It was the life that we knew. Longing for a life that can no longer be becomes easier than where we find ourselves now—transported into a strange and scary world where nothing makes sense. We've fallen through Alice's looking glass, where up is down and down is up. So instead of moving forward into a life of new possibilities, our fear keeps us rooted in the past. We welcome the darkness of our sorrow—it cloaks us and becomes our refuge. But if we're not careful, and if we stay in this comfort zone for too long, we may discover that it is indeed a very difficult place to leave.

"A comfort zone is a beautiful place, but nothing ever grows there."
Unknown

Many of us believe that if we move, even in the slightest, away from our grief and toward the light that is life, we are somehow betraying our lost loved one or sanctioning their passing. In order to move past this feeling of guilt, we must shine the light of love and self-compassion on ourselves and reach a place of knowing—that although our loved one's life in this physical plane has ended, we are still here. Our short, precious lives are calling us forward.

That said, moving forward can be fraught with hurdles. One involves the true nature of our relationship with the departed. If they loved us and were supportive of us in life, then there's a great chance that we will feel their love and encouragement from beyond. But what if while they lived, they displayed jealousy, envy, possessiveness, or anger toward us? In this case, we may be burdened with additional guilt as we struggle to carry on, because we believe they continue to harbor resentment and hostility from beyond and would object to us moving forward without them. In any case, we must not allow our loved one to continue to dictate, influence, or control our lives from the other side. They are no longer here. We are. Life moves on whether we like it or not—and whether *they* like it or not!

I was fortunate with regard to this hurdle. I knew that as in life, Charlie wished for nothing more than my happiness. In fact, he said as much in his letter to me. His words were a gift. Here is an excerpt: "One more important thing, I really hope that life becomes full of joy again for you someday. You deserve it!! Please know that the most wonderful thing you could do for my memory is to live life again. And, if it is ever possible to find a loving relationship, my sincerest wish is that you could have that love and companionship again and live a long and loving life. Again, you deserve that Best Buddy."

I wish I could tell you that knowing I had the full love and support of my deceased husband vanquished any burden of guilt I carried as I struggled to move forward and find joy again. But I can't. Not because I didn't cherish and appreciate every word he wrote—I did! But the thought of *ever* again wanting, let alone finding, another loving relationship was nowhere within my purview, especially so soon after losing him.

There's a saying that we plan and God laughs. Well, He had Himself a pretty good laugh at my expense. He waited a mere five months after Charlie died before deciding, in His infinite wisdom, to deliver me into the arms and heart of another man. To say that I was totally unprepared for this is an understatement, but this is how the path of moving forward was laid out for me.

A Different Kind of Hurdle

We're all familiar with the saying, "Timing is everything." And yes, this union with another man came too quickly on the heels of my profound loss. But I firmly believed then, as I do now, that God has a purpose for everything that unfolds. One of the affirmations that hung on my refrigerator early on was, "Allow all to unfold as it should. Trust all will unfold as it should. Surrender to all that unfolds. Accept all that unfolds." As I grieved, I made a concerted effort to uphold those tenets. To allow. To trust. To surrender. To accept.

My daily walks, especially in the first months of my healing, were enormously helpful in lifting me out of myself and easing the almost unbearable pain. I began noticing, early on and almost daily, another figure walking toward me down the sidewalk on the opposite side of the street. This person, a man, was easy to spot because he wore brightly colored T-shirts, mostly turquoise. As immersed as I was in my grieving during those walks, if I looked up and saw the color turquoise heading my way, I couldn't help smiling. I began to take some comfort, as fleeting as it was, in looking up from the sidewalk and being able to greet a passing fellow human being with a wave and a smile, and have them wave and smile back.

Those moments became very meaningful, because they lifted me out of myself and helped me to feel plugged back into the world, into humanity. I found them restorative, as they instilled within me hope for a brighter future. I had even given the man a name: Fellow Traveler, or FT for short. God continually and consistently placed FT on that sidewalk at the same time of day as me. If I walked in the morning, there he'd be. If I walked in the early afternoon, there he'd be. If I walked in the early evening hours, there he'd be. Sometimes he wasn't walking at all, but as I walked by, I would spot him sitting on a bench by the pond or sitting under a tree in the park, his face always turned away from me. On the rare occasion when I would miss him on my walk, I'd pass him in my car on my way to run errands while he was walking, in which case I'd beep my horn and wave. It was uncanny—so much so that I shared this with my sisters, my mom, and a couple of friends. FT would tell me later that he was as mystified as I was and had spoken to his family and friends as well about the serendipitous nature of our encounters.

This almost daily connection with FT those first several months lifted my spirits. Then came multiple days in a row where I didn't see him. No more turquoise T-shirt heading my way. No more waves. No more smiles. I was surprised by the depth of sadness I felt as the weeks rolled by and I didn't see him. I guessed that he'd moved or gotten a job, and I thanked God for the brief time that He'd placed FT on my path. And going back to my affirmation, I knew that his absence was meant to be, that I needed to "accept all that unfolds." God had His reasons, and I trusted, as always, that He knew best.

It was a little over a month since I'd last seen FT, and five months without Charlie, when I returned home one Friday from a visit back East to see my mom and one of my best friends. I was in a very bad way, and coming home to an empty house triggered an episode of acute grief. On Sunday morning, I found myself kneeling on my bedroom floor, sobbing and imploring both God and Charlie to tell me why … why this horrible, tragic loss had happened to me. I cried so hard that my tear ducts dried up.

Since the tears refused to flow, I decided to take a shower to pull myself together. It was a beautiful, late summer's day, but I was far too distraught and exhausted to even contemplate taking a walk. After showering, I gazed out of my office window, which overlooks a fairly small section of the sidewalk across the street. As I stood there mindlessly flossing my teeth, of all things, my swollen eyes caught a glimpse of turquoise. I looked closer. I couldn't believe it. It was FT. Suddenly, I heard Charlie's voice as clear as day saying, "Go to him. He can help you."

Without a moment's hesitation, in lightning speed, I donned my walking gear, bolted out my front door, and began running down the sidewalk in an attempt to catch up with him. By the time I did, FT was sitting under his favorite tree in the park, his back to me. I just walked up behind him and said, "Hey, fellow traveler, where have you been?" To which he turned, looked at me, and replied, "Where have YOU been?" And that is how we finally met face-to-face.

The connection we made was instantaneous and deep. Very early into our conversation that morning, we both knew instinctively that our coming together was for a purpose and had been divinely orchestrated. There was no other explanation that we could come up with that explained our passing each other at different times on different days almost daily for months.

Sadly, our fairy tale beginning would not enjoy a fairy tale ending. FT was acutely aware that I was a newly minted widow who was in the early stages of grieving a significant loss, one that had occurred in a tragic and traumatic way. And that "way," Charlie's suicide, had stirred up other feelings and emotions that even caught me unaware—and they seemed to be triggered by my engagement in this new, romantic union. I was crippled by feelings of guilt, shame, resentment, and unworthiness, feelings that many suicide survivors are burdened with. These feelings compounded my grief and drastically impaired my ability to remain consistent in my relationship with FT. As much as he tried his best to love me through my grief, my "allowing" him to do just that—and to love him in return in all the ways required to establish and maintain a loving relationship—became a herculean task for me. For the duration of our relationship, I became a container for his love and empathy, and he became a container for my pain.

Meeting FT and committing to a relationship had brought me too quickly to a crossroad. The thought of walking headlong into this unknown territory absolutely terrified me. I would make my way down the road a little, with him, timidly and with great trepidation, only to freak out time and again. And even though I knew the past was no longer real and no longer an option, I would run as fast as I could back to it. The past was the road of "safety," and I sought refuge in something that no longer existed. And then I would push FT as far away from me as I could.

As terrified as I was to fall through Alice's looking glass yet again—back down into that strange and scary world where down was up and up was down—that's exactly where I found myself. Except that now I was living not in one but *two* equally strange and scary worlds: a world without Charlie and a world with FT. I straddled both for a very long time.

My desperate attempts to navigate through my grief over the loss of Charlie and my feelings for someone new cast a nightmarish pall over my life, the likes of which I had never experienced. I felt that God was truly testing me. I also firmly believed at the time, and still do, that Charlie had no objections to my being with this man. But that didn't stop me from feeling as though I was being disloyal to him and his memory. And admitting to myself that I had *any* romantic feelings for another man so soon after Charlie's passing was, in my mind, the ultimate betrayal of him and of the deep and abiding love that we'd shared for over two decades, despite what he had wished for me in his letter.

I had never been more conflicted in my life than I was then. I find it interesting, in hindsight, that *Charlie* felt I was deserving of a new life and a new love, but *I* didn't believe I was! Again, this is an example of my feelings of unworthiness that I was burdened with for quite a long time.

FT and I were together and apart, back and forth more than a tennis ball at Wimbledon. This proved to be emotionally and physically exhausting for us both, but especially for him. He even left the state for six months until I asked him to try yet again. And we did. But I subconsciously established a cycle with him whereby I could only remain with him for, at most, two weeks; as soon as I allowed myself to be fully open and loving with him, I would panic, and this overwhelming need to push him as far away from me as possible would consume me. My incessant reeling him in, only to release him days or weeks later, was not healthy for either one of us and caused us both deep anguish and heartache.

When I reluctantly pushed him away for the last time, more than three years after I had first said hello to him under that tree in the park, FT shared with me his perspective on our often loving but equally tumultuous time together. He felt that for nearly the entire time we were in relationship, it was as though I had been wearing a pair of glasses that were etched with Charlie on the lenses. Any time I looked at FT, I saw Charlie and my life with *him* and only small tidbits of

FT. On the infrequent occasions when I was ready, willing, and able to remove those glasses and put them away, only then was I able to see FT clearly and with a loving, open, and vulnerable heart. But those glasses were never far from my reach, and sooner rather than later, they would make their way back up to my face again, and I'd panic and push FT away.

This cycle repeated itself over and over and over. Also sadly, when those glasses were on, I began projecting all of my unresolved feelings of anger, abandonment, and betrayal onto FT, a man who was only trying to love me. It wasn't pretty, and it wasn't fair; in fact, it was downright tragic. But it was what it was. In the end, I was simply unable to put those glasses away for good and to consistently keep my heart open to loving and being loved by him. Releasing FT for good proved excruciating and heartbreaking.

God had brought us together, not for all time, but for a time—during the darkest and most difficult period of my life. He had asked me to move forward well before I was ready to—before I had even reached many of the necessary steps on the grief journey that typically precede and prepare us for a new relationship. While His reasoning sometimes confounded me, today I have come to not only understand it, but also be deeply grateful for His divine wisdom.

And so divine wisdom decided to give me the gift of FT. This gift, this blessing of my FT in his turquoise T-shirt, was and will remain one of the greatest blessings of my life. He was the key that opened the gate of my imprisoned, shattered heart and set it free. And it was through the power of his love for me that he began gluing the million shattered pieces of it back together.

Still I wonder: What if I had met FT when my heart was wholly and completely open for business instead of when it was so deeply wounded? Would we have gotten our fairy tale ending? I will never know. But for what it's worth, the piece of my heart that his deep love and our love together managed to open will forever be his. And although our paths diverged, I will forever cherish the distance we walked together, hand in hand.

"At times, our own light goes out and is rekindled by a spark from another person. Each of us has cause to think with deep gratitude of those who have lighted the flame within us."
Albert Schweitzer

Another hurdle we encounter when we lose a loved one is the scrutiny of other people—our closest family and friends and then those outside of that circle who knew the deceased. It's human nature, but it seems that everyone has their own opinions, notions, expectations, judgments, and ideas about grieving and how "best" to do it. We may feel that all eyes are on us and that our lives are being dissected under a microscope as we move through our grieving process. And sometimes, in an effort to be pleasing—most especially to our immediate family members and closest friends—we may subjugate what and how we're feeling, or make choices contrary to what our hearts are telling us, because we don't want to disappoint anyone by behaving in a way that might deviate from their expectations.

If we find ourselves toeing the line for the benefit of others rather than making choices that benefit ourselves, we must pause, go within, and remember that grieving our loss is *our* journey and ours *alone*, and how we wish to take that journey is up to us. My yoga instructor begins each practice with words that are just as applicable to grieving: "Remember, there is no competition, no judgments, and no expectations. All that matters is what happens on your own mat. This is your journey." And so it is.

My relationship with FT serves as a perfect example. At first, my family and friends were extremely happy for me. Like me, they were mystified and intrigued by our frequent, serendipitous encounters while walking and couldn't help but ascribe the same some sort of Universal or Divine intention to them. And they all knew how devastated I was over losing Charlie, and were supportive and encouraging of *anything* that would ease my suffering even in the slightest. Also, I discovered that grief can be symbiotic. If I felt better, this encouraged my family and friends to feel better.

When I shared with everyone how I had introduced myself to FT, they were elated. But it wouldn't take long for them to change their tune. My constant yo-yoing with him, which began very early on, understandably caused great concern and consternation among my friends and family, at times causing deep rifts between them and me when they disagreed with certain choices I made. I began to feel that everyone was watching me—gauging me to see if the decisions I made as to how to live my life, especially with regard to my new relationship, would align with theirs.

To top it off, I'm a people-pleaser. I had always put too much stock in what others, especially my immediate family and closest friends, thought of me. And because they had all showered me with their deep love, sympathy, and compassion when Charlie died, I felt a heightened sense of gratitude and loyalty to them, along with a heightened fear of disappointing them if I made choices that were contrary to theirs and for which they might judge me as I moved forward in my life.

My fear of displeasing others—or worse, of being judged or invalidated by them—held great sway early on in my relationship with FT and often caused me to make decisions that were contrary to what my heart was telling me to do, decisions that invariably broke both our hearts time and again. Eventually, because of the repeated on-again, off-again nature of our relationship, it didn't take long before everyone around me grew exhausted by all the drama.

But, as we who grieve come to know, our grief transforms us. I was not the same person I was before I lost Charlie. As my faith and trust in God and Universe deepened, so did my courage and resolve. And as I healed and learned and grew through my grieving, I began making choices—sometimes hard ones and admittedly, in hindsight, some pretty wrongheaded ones—that I knew in my heart were aligned with *my* truth at the time, rather than what others approved of. This related to every aspect of my life as it was unfolding: how I chose to grieve, how I chose to heal, and how I chose to engage again in the outside world. Standing and remaining in my truth was one of the most difficult but most transformational, pivotal, and valuable life lessons I have ever learned. Sometimes what I believe to be right for me isn't necessarily what someone else believes to be right for me, and I'm perfectly okay with that now.

That said, even as I was in the process of writing this chapter, I shot off an email to my editor and fellow author, Laurie Viera Rigler, seeking her advice and opinion with regard to my fear of the possibility of being judged by you, my reader, if I disclosed that I met someone so soon after Charlie passed. This is an excerpt of her very wise reply: "It's a common human pitfall to always want people to like us and approve of us. But it never happens. Not as a person living her life. Not as an author. You and I and everyone else in this world are never going to please and satisfy everyone. There is nothing you can do to stop that. What you can do is marshal your strength with every method at your command and not let the judgments and projections win. Easier said than done, but believe me, it's essential."

This is wisdom for the ages and applies not only to how we choose to live our lives, but how we choose to grieve. I can't overstate this enough: Our journey through grief is *our own*. As for me, when I was finally ready, willing, and able to make the shift from worrying about what others thought to simply listening to my own heart, I began taking baby steps in what lies beyond the last signpost of Acceptance: The Rest of My Life.

This is the last part of my journal entry from above: "Point me in the other direction, sweetie. Help me turn my face to the now and not back to the then. Help me to be brave. Help me to embrace fully and with gusto, the rest of my life. Help me get to a place where I want my life and future more desperately than I miss you."

I can share with you the exact date when I arrived at that "place." It was on November 8, 2017, two years and seven months, almost to the day, after Charlie's death. Up to this point, I was still feeling directionless. Charlie and I had worked together over the years in a number of business ventures. When he passed, we'd been working as franchise brokers, helping folks find their perfect franchise or business opportunity. While it had been fulfilling in its way, I knew immediately that it was not something I wished to continue doing without him. Added to that was the fact that my grief was so all-encompassing and profound I could scarcely think straight, let alone return to the demands of running a business.

I have a daily prayer practice wherein I ask God how I can best serve Him. I offer myself up to Him as His instrument, and I ask Him to use me for His and my greatest good. I pray that He make it clear to me always what I am supposed to be doing with my life as I continue to move forward. I began this practice very soon after my loss. In those early days, I knew how much various healers had helped me in my time of need, and I began getting a strong sense that God was telling me that I was to become a healer in some capacity, although I had no idea how that was going to manifest.

One day, as I was browsing the Internet, I happened upon the website for the University of Metaphysical Sciences. I was intrigued by their diverse curriculum and began taking their online courses in hopes that my studies would lead me to one particular modality of healing that would most resonate with me. As fascinating as the courses were, nothing was "speaking" to me or, more importantly, to my heart.

My prayers then led me, in September 2017, to seek out and find Nancy, a gifted therapist and life coach. It was during my session with her on November 8, 2017, that Nancy asked me what I believed my God-given gifts or talents were. I immediately said, "Writing." She then asked, "What are you doing about that?" I told her I'd written a novel that I wasn't particularly happy with a number of years back, and then I told her about a book project that Charlie and I had begun in the mid-1990s but had shelved after working on it for two years. When I shared the concept of the book, a nonfiction anthology about the 1960s, she got very excited. In talking with her, so did I! I think I'd known all along that I was meant to be writing again, but other than journaling, I hadn't acted on it.

Upon returning home that day, I rushed upstairs to my office, sat on my floor, and began pulling out and reviewing all the files relevant to "The 60s Project." For the first time in a long, long time, I felt almost joyful. As I pulled out one manila folder, a piece of paper, folded in half, floated from it and landed squarely on my lap. I picked up the paper and saw that it was a note that I'd written back in the mid-'90s—a note that a much younger Karen had written to her future self; a note that I was meant to find again, that I *needed* to find and read in that *exact* moment, after close to 25 years. While one side of the note related to the 1960s project, the other side had no bearing on the topic at all yet was far more important. The note, which has been hanging on the wall in my office since that day, reads: "Cast your butterfly net. Be open to thrilling new opportunities and possibilities. Try to look beyond this point and see what lies ahead for you. Keep your eye on the stars and everything else will follow."

I was amazed! I *knew* instantly that this was clear confirmation from God that I was on the right path. That day, I had resurrected a book project and God had resurrected me. Upon reading those words, I felt my life force energy surge throughout my body and the heavy shroud of grief that had been weighing on me for so long suddenly lift. I felt lighter, and I had clarity—about everything: past, present, and future.

And so I began writing. I spent a few weeks diligently and gleefully working on breathing life back into "The 60s Project." But God had other plans for me, because my heart began to speak with a clarity and surety I couldn't ignore— it was compelling me to put that project aside for a while, and to first write about my journey through grief and loss. I listened and immediately acted on what I had heard.

Writing *Love Loss Light* reignited my passion for life and infused it with purpose and meaning. It was the rope that tethered me back to the world. Admittedly, the process of writing this book was extremely cathartic, but most important, it fulfilled my intense desire to offer in a meaningful way, a measure of comfort and healing to others who, like me, had experienced profound loss. This book was both an inspiration and aspiration. It was my lifesaver. It helped point me in the other direction. It helped me to turn my face to the now and not back to the then. It helped me to be brave. It helped me to embrace, fully and with gusto, the rest of my life. It got me to that place where I wanted my life and future more desperately than I missed Charlie. And finally, it was proof positive, along with the miracle of having been graced early on with the experience of trying my hand and heart at love again, that "more good things await me."

I will always think of November 8, 2017, as sacred, a day of resurrection. On that day, I found myself standing on "the threshold between loss and revelation," which author Francis Weller speaks of in his book by the same name (which he co-created with author and artist Rashani Réa). On that day, my long, arduous journey through grief had delivered me straight into the arms of God. And God, in turn, had delivered me from my pain and suffering by sparking new life into me and restoring my confidence that I could, once again, breathe on my own. He had given me the motivation and the courage to move forward and to embrace a future without my beloved Charlie by my side.

I had reached the summit of my grief journey, and instead of looking over my shoulder from whence I came and asking "Why?" I found myself looking ahead, to that point where the line of the earth's surface and the sky appear to meet, and asking, "Why not?" New horizons beckoned. My heart was telling me that I had honored Charlie in grief. I had grieved for him deeply, fully, and well, but now it was time for me to honor him in life—by living the rest of mine deeply, fully, and well. That is what I plan to do. He wished for nothing less.

"It was not my choice to survive without you...so I choose to live and to honor you. I am still standing."
Unknown

After loss, we owe it—if not to our lost loved one, then to ourselves—to embrace life fully and completely again, however that looks for each of us. It takes time and great courage to reach for the light that will illuminate the path ahead. It takes even greater courage to leave the sanctuary of our grief and step fully into that light. But even the longest, darkest tunnel has a light at either end. This is our biggest test thus far on our journey. When we come to the end of our tunnel, will we be ready to leave its safety and step fully into the light? Will we allow the light to infuse us with life? Will we allow the light to eradicate any lingering darkness in our hearts? Will we allow our grief to alchemize us? Or will we retreat back into the comfort of the darkness? Will our loss close our hearts so tightly that we find it difficult, if not impossible, to open our hearts and be vulnerable again? Remembering that we *are* the choices we make, what will we choose for ourselves when we arrive at our final destination beyond the last signpost, The Rest of Our Lives?

"Someday, in retrospect, your years of struggle will strike you as the most beautiful."
Sigmund Freud

One day, we wounded warriors will return from our dark days in exile. We will have grown tired and weary with fatigue after a long and mighty battle, and we will leave this battle behind. What we will carry forward in our hearts is the reason we fought in the first place. We will carry our undying love for the one who has died—for them and for all who went before them and to all who will come after. We will return home a different person than the one who'd set off to war. Our time away, in the interior world, will have imbued within us greater wisdom, courage, forgiveness, acceptance, allowance, and gratitude—and far more love and compassion for ourselves, for others, and for our world than we ever dreamed possible. We will reach for that light, and we will turn it on. And we will bask once again in the glory of life.

"You've seen my descent. Now watch my rising"
Rumi

***

We begin our arduous journey through grief and loss having been left behind. We end our journey having learned how to live life again without the presence of our loved one in it. Life calls us forward, and sooner or later, each of us heeds the call. But as we move forward into embracing life again, we may feel as though it is we who are now leaving our cherished dead behind. We also know that grief has been our greatest teacher. It has taught us, and we have learned its lessons well: That we never lost them and they never lost us. That we are tethered together for eternity. That the remains of the day are love and memories, the true ties that bind—eternal and infinite. Ever-existing and undying. That love leaves behind far more than death can ever take away. That we carry them deep within our hearts where they will reside every moment for all time. Just listen. They're right here. Amen.

Going Forward

Today I removed the rearview mirror from my van.
It's been dangling there taunting me for too long.
Have you ever baked a cake,
and forgot to add the eggs,
or added too much water?
And found it cracked
when you pulled it from the oven?
And tried to paste it back
together with frosting?
And the more you tried
to fix it, the more it would crumble?
There is no going back.
Eggs can't be added to a baked cake.
Remove the mirror.
Eat the cake.
Drive on.

Suzette Winona Summers, 2014

15

The Rest of Our Lives

"There is nothing more beautiful than the mantle of survivor. There is nothing more illuminated than the resurrected body, the new personality that emerges when the old one has been laid to rest."
Marianne Williamson, The Gift of Change

WE EACH BEGIN OUR JOURNEY through grief and loss by laying our loved one to rest. For me, I have come to know that on the day Charlie died, I died too. As he was resurrected in the world beyond the veil, so too was I here on the physical plane.

We each arrive on the other side of the doorway of our pain and suffering completely transformed. We are not the same person we were before our journey began, nor could we be. Nor should we be. Nor would we want to be. We have traveled headlong into the unknown, and the wounds we sustained while there are sacred. They have made us who we are today and who we will be for the rest of our lives: survivors.

So much falls away from us when we lose someone we love. We are forced to take a journey into the unknown, leaving all that was familiar behind. But that journey calls forth endless opportunities to refill and replenish ourselves mind, body, and spirit. If we can surrender ourselves to it completely, grief and our personal journeys through it can transmute our pain and suffering into aliveness and awakening, and enrich the rest of our lives in ways we never dreamed possible. On the day we lost our loved one, our heart may have been burned empty, but we discover that now it can contain the whole world and that the sorrows that have crippled us have given us wings.

"What once felt like grief is now the very substance of these open wings."
Rashani Réa, The Threshold Between Loss and Revelation

May You . . .

Choose, move, move on, change, grow, adjust, embrace, acknowledge, and mourn.
Let go, explore, empower, accept, remember, give thanks, surrender, and be courageous.
Laugh, cry, trust, understand, discover, wonder, praise, pray, compliment, and encourage.
Discuss, commiserate, absorb, listen, ponder, reflect, evolve, hope, support, and have faith.
Create, give, forgive, receive, inspire, cherish, teach, learn, share, impart, let it be, and become.
Lose, gain, thrive, carry on, play, age gracefully, celebrate, find peace, and be joyful, kind, compassionate, and passionate.
Love, live, dance, sing, dream, imagine, believe, hold on to your power, be kind to yourself, be patient, rise up, and soar!

Karen Trench, 2003

A Note from Me to You

Thank you for allowing me to share my journey with you. I am deeply humbled, honored, and grateful. Please know that in this moment, I am surrounding you with light, love, compassion, and admiration. And may you *never* forget: You are stronger than you think and you *will* survive!

"Death does not exceed our strength."
Rainer Maria Rilke

Birdwings

"Your grief for what you've lost lifts a mirror
up to where you're bravely working.
Expecting the worst, you look, and instead,
here's the joyful face you've been wanting to see.
Your hand opens and closes and opens and closes.
If it were always a fist or always stretched open,
you would be paralyzed.
Your deepest presence
is in every small contracting and expanding,
the two beautifully balanced and coordinated
as birdwings."

Rumi

Karen Trench

Appreciations

To my mom, Eleanore Bandecchi, and my sisters, Priscilla Cole and Kathleen Leach, for their unwavering and unconditional love and support. They are my earth angels.

To my dad Edwin Leach, who left us too soon, for instilling within me his passion for words, both written and spoken. He is greatly missed.

To Aaron, Christine, and Austin Trench for the tears, the laughter, and the love shared mostly around my kitchen table. They bring immeasurable joy to my life.

To my brother-in-law, Tom Trench, for all he did to help me when I was most helpless—from providing free lawn care to selling Charlie's beloved truck "Lucky" to assisting me with business and estate matters early on and, most importantly, for bringing Charlie home to me.

To my niece, Meghan Burke, for finding the perfect massage therapist in that first week, for staying with me for weeks at a time and driving me, her very own "Miss Daisy," around town, and for going above and beyond the call of duty by offering to spoon with me in bed in those early days of profound grief and loss.

To my brother, Bill Leach, for reminding me that sometimes our loved ones feel compelled to leave us before they actually leave the world. I am grateful to him for having taught me the important lessons of how to honor, release, and accept those things that we would rather not have to.

To my brother, Ed Leach. Even though he lives halfway around the world, we have enjoyed many deep and meaningful discussions by phone, which have gone a long way in keeping him close in my heart. I am graced by the presence of each of these family members in my life.

To all of my amazing, beautiful friends who wrapped me in their arms and basked me in their light and love during my darkest days and beyond.

To Sheryl Allen, Pam Malloy, Rita Burke, Sam Reynolds, Lisa Brunner, Susan Nicholaou, Eve Altieri, Grace Oringer, Gail Brill, Gloria Reeder, Lisa Pinney-Keusch, Heather Gunther, Diane Carnall, Sherri Rose-Walker, and Cynde Denson—each one enriches and beautifies my life. To Lisa Brunner I would like to add that I will be forever grateful for her gift of "the field." To Sheryl Allen I would like to acknowledge with my most heartfelt gratitude everything she did for me and for Charlie to bring to fruition on a grand scale, the wedding that we'd always envisioned and for doing the same when it came time to honor and celebrate his life. I don't know what I would have done without her love, her friendship and her extraordinary organizational skills on either of these most sacred, solemn occasions.

To my sisters-in-law, Sharon Bankes, Debbie Trench, and Ingrid Leach, whom I thank from the bottom of my heart for every kind gesture of love and support both big and small.

To my Auntie Pat (Priscilla) Mongillo for every butterfly kiss she sent me in her greeting cards and for every original poem she included within each of them. She and they brought me many moments of joy in my despair.

To my guardian angels, Elsie, Beverly and Ellen. I feel your love surrounding me and hear your whispered words of encouragement daily.

To my furry pals Fumo and Smudge for their companionship, unconditional love, and silly antics that made me laugh, sometimes even through my tears.

To Robert "RJ" Renneker and Colin "Bones" Jones for their friendship and devotion to Charlie and for gracing me with the same after he passed.

To fellow author and my and Charlie's wonderful friend and neighbor at altitude, Alex Drummond, for every heartfelt, homemade greeting card he sent me after Charlie died, and for the moving and empathetic words contained therein. Each bolstered my spirit immensely and seemed to appear in my mailbox exactly when I was in desperate need of a boost.

To the wide array of gifted healers who were brought forth on my journey in the most miraculous ways. I feel so blessed to have crossed their paths. I am especially grateful to Tricia McCannon, Donna Morrish, Aurelia Taylor, Walter Zajac, Nancy Harris, Laura Lounello, and finally, to Charlie's and my much-loved and cherished friend, spiritual advisor, and Master Rolfer, B. Logan Kline. He celebrated our love when he married us and again when I was forced to let Charlie go and every day in between. He was one of Charlie's greatest blessings and he remains one of mine.

To the dozens of authors, too many to list, whose books on loss and grieving were literally my salvation as I began my journey through grief. I cannot thank them enough. Their words were beacons of light that illuminated my path through grief and loss and that would later inspire me to write this book. There are two authors in particular I would like to thank: Sameet M. Kumar, for his brilliant book *Grieving Mindfully* and for writing a beautiful foreword; and Kamal Ravikant, for his perfect book *Live Your Truth.* In my most desperate hours, these go-to books became my refuge.

To Sergeant Tamara Mulano of the Denver Police Department, who was then a detective and the first officer to arrive at the Denver VA hospital where Charlie died. The deep compassion and kindness she bestowed upon me and my family, not only in the early hours but even months after losing him, were welcome and cherished gifts to us all. I especially want to thank her for taking time out from her busy schedule to meet me at the hospital on the second anniversary of Charlie's passing and for bringing me to the exact location where he took his last breath. I was honored to meet her in person, to give her a big hug, and to express my deepest gratitude.

With deep gratitude and reverence to Sherri Rose-Walker, Catherine Firpo, Suzette Winona Summers, Rashani Réa, Nell Aurelia, Elizabeth Adams, and Jamie K. Reaser for allowing me the honor and privilege of including their powerful and moving poetry in this book. Each of their poems appeared in my life exactly when needed and acted like a cooling balm to my burning soul. They and their poetry are blessings to me.

A special, heartfelt thanks to my editor, Laurie Viera Rigler, for her deep compassion, honesty, feedback, and friendship. Her unwavering encouragement and belief in me and my story inspired me every step of the way, and it is because of her that both were made that much better.

And to my copyeditor, Susan Hindman. If Laurie got me down the field, Susan took me over the goal line. My dream to write the best possible memoir about my grief journey was made manifest because of these two gifted, compassionate women and their superior editing skills. I am deeply grateful.

I wish to thank Jenn Smith (HappyDolphinPress.com) for her tutelage in the world of self-publishing. Her kick-start early on provided the impetus this student needed to graduate!

To author and editor Raven Dodd (ravendodd.com) for her passion for fonts and formatting. This passion translated into a beautiful interior layout and design.

To Michael Molinet (michael-molinet.com), a wonderfully gifted author and illustrator for creating the book cover I'd imagined and for reimagining it in a way that far exceeded what I'd dreamed it could ever be.

To award winning Veronica Yager (yellowstudiosonline.com), for her extraordinary expertise in web design, social media marketing, eBook conversion, for being instrumental in getting my story into your hands and finally, for recommending Michael Molinet! My heart is full of gratitude for these talented and dedicated individuals.

And lastly, to my Fellow Traveler. I am grateful to him for more than he will ever know. I say to him now, "Never forget the thin, red thread."

Inspirations and

Permissions

Poetry

The poetry of Jalal ad-Din Muhammad Rumi from *A Year With Rumi: Daily Readings* by Coleman Barks (New York: HarperCollins, 2006); and *The Essential Rumi* by Coleman Barks (New York: HarperCollins, 1995); reprinted with permission of Coleman Barks.

"Picking Up the Pieces," from *Sacred Lines: A Personal Journey from Darkness to Light* by Elizabeth Adams (Bloomington, IN: Balboa Press, a division of Hay House, 2016); reprinted with permission of Elizabeth Adams.

"The Song of the Phoenix," by Jamie K. Reaser (http://talkingwaters-poetry.blogspot.com/2018/06/the-song-of-the-phoenix.html as to be published in the Truth and Beauty collection; reprinted with permission of Jamie K. Reaser.

The following poems are from the 2015 edition of *We'Moon—Gaia Rhythms for Women*, published by Mother Tongue Ink. Each is used with permission of the authors:

Catherine Firpo, "Bitter Sweet Resonance"

Sherri Rose-Walker, "The Wisdom of Brokenness," "Complexities of Solitude," "The Divine Simplicity of Breath," and "Return from Exile"

Nell Aurelia, "Cracked"

*Rashani Réa, "The Unbroken"

Suzette Winona Summers, "Going Forward"

* "The Unbroken" was written by Rashani Réa in December 1991 following the fifth death in her family. Her book about this poem is called *Beyond Brokenness*.

Book Passages

SACRED LINES – A PERSONAL JOURNEY FROM DARKNESS TO LIGHT by Elizabeth Adams, (Balboa Press, a division of Hay House Inc., © 2016); reprinted with permission of Elizabeth Adams.

FACING DARKNESS, FINDING LIGHT: LIFE AFTER SUICIDE (Scotland: Findhorn Press, © 2016); reprinted with permission of Steffany Barton.

A LAMP IN THE DARKNESS, © 2011, 2014 Jack Kornfield, excerpted with permission of publisher, Sounds True, Inc.

MINDFUL INTENTIONS by Louie Schwartzberg and MIRAVAL, (Hay House Publishing, 2015); reprinted with permission of Hay House Publishing.

THE GIFT OF CHANGE: SPIRITUAL GUIDANCE FOR LIVING YOUR BEST LIFE by Marianne Williamson, (Harper Collins Publishers, 2004); reprinted with permission of Harper Collins Publishers.

Additional quotes interwoven throughout this book are by *Rashani Réa, *Francis Weller, *Alfred K. LaMotte *Jamie K. Reaser, *Mirabai Starr, *Matthew Fox, Hilary Stanton Zunin and Leonard Zunin, Steve Maraboli, Elizabeth Adams, Starhawk, Tricia McCannon, Laurie Viera Rigler, Albert Schweitzer, Elizabeth Watson, Natalie Costanza-Chavez, Susan Griffin, Susan Powers, Buddha, Sigmund Freud, Kathryn Walker, Isak Dinesen, Bhagavad-Gita, The Holy Bible, Kahlil Gibran, William Shakespeare, Washington Irving, Tao Te Ching, Lao Tzu, Pablo Neruda, Mother Teresa, Louise Hay, Attar of Nishapur, Rainer Maria Rilke, Sononfu E. Somé, Winston Churchill, William Penn.

*Quotes as published in *The Threshold Between Loss and Revelation* by Rashani Réa: (rashani.com) and Francis Weller: (francisweller.net) Alfred K. LaMotte: (http://thebelovedwithin.blogspot.com/), **Jamie K. Reaser: (hiraethpress.com/Jamie-k-reaser), Mirabai Starr: (mirabaistarr.com), Matthew Fox: (matthewfox.org).

** Jamie K. Reaser's quote, "Glory to the Phoenix," comes from her poem, "The Rising Times," published (2011) in *Note to Self: Poems for Changing the World from the Inside Out*, Hiraeth Press, Danvers, MA.

The publisher has made every effort to clear all reprint permissions not deemed "fair use" for this book. If any required acknowledgements have been omitted, it is unintentional. If notified, the publisher will be pleased to rectify any omission in future editions.

Karen Trench

About the Author

Karen Trench never imagined that she would give up a successful career in television for anything, let alone for a log cabin high in the Colorado Rockies. Then again, she never thought she'd meet her soul mate, with whom she lived in those mountains, on and off, for two decades of blissful marriage. When she found herself a widow, a shocked survivor of her husband's death, she could not have conceived that she would someday emerge from the wreckage a strong, happy, and emotionally empowered woman. Now she shares her story of *Love Loss Light* with a fervent prayer that it may be of service to her fellow travelers in grief. Her journey continues at www.karentrench.com.

58286202R00138

Made in the USA
Columbia, SC
21 May 2019